SELF-DECEPTION UNMASKED

SELF-DECEPTION UNMASKED

Alfred R. Mele

PRINCETON UNIVERSITY PRESS

PRINCETON AND OXFORD

Published by Princeton University Press, 41 William Street,
Princeton, New Jersey 08540
In the United Kingdom: Princeton University Press,
3 Market Place, Woodstock, Oxfordshire OX20 1SY

Library of Congress Cataloging-in-Publication Data

Mele, Alfred R., 1951–
Self-deception unmasked / Alfred R. Mele.
p. cm. — (Princeton monographs in philosophy)
Includes bibliographical references and index.
ISBN 0-691-05744-3 (hardcover : alk. paper)—
ISBN 0-691-05745-1 (pbk. : alk. paper)
ISBN-13: 978-0-691-05745-3
1. Self-deception. I. Title. II. Series.
BD439 .M45 2000
128′.3—dc21 00-032626

This book has been composed in Janson Text and Centaur

www.pup.princeton.edu

Printed in the United States of America

1 3 5 7 9 10 8 6 4 2

For my father, Al

Contents

Preface

WHAT MOTIVATED ME to accept Harry Frankfurt's kind invitation to submit a manuscript to this series was the opportunity to present and defend in a systematic way a position on self-deception that has evolved partly out of my earlier attempts to shed light on the phenomenon. Although I draw on previously published work, the defense offered here of my central theses about the kind of self-deception that has received pride of place in the philosophical and psychological literature is much more robust and has an important new dimension that benefits from recent empirical work on hypothesis testing. The general position on self-deception advanced here also is considerably more comprehensive than what I have been able to manage in my scattered efforts on the topic over the years.

I have been thinking about self-deception longer than it pleases me to acknowledge. My first stab at the topic (Mele 1982), a brief commentary on a provocative paper by Robert Audi (1982), contains some of the seeds of the position advanced in this book. My central point there was that "there is no close general analogy between self-deception and *intentional* other deception" and that "when our attachment to this analogy is broken, there is significantly less motivation to postulate unconscious [true] beliefs in ordinary cases of self-deception" (Mele 1982, p. 164). In Mele 1983, I offered a more rigorous defense of this point, a statement of characteristic and jointly sufficient conditions for self-deception, and a resolution of the "static" puzzle about self-deception highlighted in Chapter 1. That article was the basis for Chapter 9 of *Irrationality* (Mele 1987a). Another chapter of *Irrationality* also tackled self-deception: in Chapter 10, drawing on some literature in social psychology, I offered a resolution of a puzzle about the dynamics of self-deception. These two chapters are a partial basis for two recent articles, Mele 1998b and Mele 1997a. The former was written as an invited contribution to a 1993 interdisciplinary conference on self-deception at Stanford University organized by Jean-Pierre Dupuy and subsequently published in a volume containing several of the papers presented there. Owing to the nature of the invitation, I was not bashful about borrowing from *Irrationality*, but I did branch out in two directions. I made use of new empirical literature that supported a central hypothesis about motivationally biased belief advanced in *Irrationality* and, at Dupuy's request, I examined a literary example of self-deception. (My discussion in Chapter 3 of Isaac Bashevis Singer's short story "Gimpel the Fool" derives partly from that paper.) Some time after the Stanford conference, I was invited to submit a target article to *Behavioral and Brain Sciences*. That article (Mele 1997a) is a wider-ranging and more heavily empirical descendant of the conference paper. It benefited from two rounds of revision prompted by fifteen referee reports.

In this book, I have borrowed liberally from published work of mine. Parts of Chapter 1 derive from three sources: "Real Self-Deception," *Behavioral and Brain Sciences* 20 (1997): 91–102 (Mele 1997a); my reply to the *BBS* commentaries, "Understanding and Explaining Real Self-Deception," *Behavioral and Brain Sciences* 20 (1997): 127–34 (Mele 1997b); and "Motivated Belief and Agency," *Philosophical Psychology* 11 (1998): 353–69 (Mele 1998a). Parts of Chapter 2 derive from Mele 1997a, Mele 1998a, and another article: "Twisted Self-Deception," *Philosophical Psychology* 12 (1999): 117–37 (Mele 1999a).[1] Parts of

Chapter 3 derive from the same three articles as Chapter 1 and an additional source: "Two Paradoxes of Self-Deception," in J. Dupuy, ed., *Self-Deception and Paradoxes of Rationality* (Stanford: CSLI, 1998), pp. 37–58 (Mele 1998b). Parts of Chapter 4 derive from the same three sources as Chapter 1. Chapter 5 is based on Mele 1999a.

Naturally, I have learned from authors of published responses to my previous work on self-deception. For useful informal discussion and written remarks, I am grateful to Robert Audi, Kent Bach, Jim Friedrich, Rainer Reisenzein, and Bill Talbott. I also have benefited from the advice of two anonymous referees.

I completed the final revision of this book during my tenure of a 1999–2000 NEH Fellowship for College Teachers. (The fellowship supported work on another book—tentatively entitled *Motivation and Agency*—that is well underway at the time of this writing.) Much of the revision was accomplished while I was a Visiting Fellow in the Philosophy Program in the Research School of Social Sciences at the Australian National University (June through August, 1999). I am grateful to the NEH and the ANU for their support, and to Davidson College for a 1999–2000 sabbatical leave.

SELF-DECEPTION UNMASKED

I

Introduction: Approaches, Puzzles, Biases, and Agency

"A SURVEY of university professors found that 94% thought they were better at their jobs than their average colleague" (Gilovich 1991, p. 77). Are university professors exceptionally adept at self-deception? Perhaps not. "A survey of one million high school seniors found that . . . *all* students thought they were above average" in their "ability to get along with others . . . and 25% thought they were in the top 1%" (ibid.). One might suspect that the respondents to these surveys were not being entirely sincere in their answers. Then again, how many university professors do you know who do *not* think that they are better at what they do than their average colleague?

Data such as these suggest that we sometimes deceive ourselves. That suggestion raises some interesting questions. How do we deceive ourselves? Why do we deceive ourselves? What is it to deceive oneself? Is self-deception even possible? These questions guide my discussion in this book.

Some theorists understand self-deception as largely isomorphic with stereotypical interpersonal deception. This understanding, which has generated some much discussed puzzles or "paradoxes," guides influential work on self-deception not only in philosophy but also in psychology, psychiatry, and biology.[1] In the course of resolving the major puzzles, I argue that the attempt to understand self-deception on the model of stereotypical interpersonal deception is fundamentally misguided. The position on self-deception defended here is *deflationary*. If I am right, self-deception is neither irresolvably paradoxical nor mysterious, and it is explicable without the assistance of mental exotica. Although a theorist whose interest in self-deception is restricted to the outer limits of logical or conceptual possibility might view this as draining the topic of conceptual intrigue, the main source of broader, enduring interest in self-deception is a concern to understand and explain the behavior of real human beings.

1. Preview

Self-deception apparently occurs in two quite different forms, "straight" and "twisted." Straight cases of self-deception have received pride of place in philosophical and empirical work. In these cases, people are self-deceived in believing something that they want to be true—for example, that they are not seriously ill, that their children are not experimenting with drugs, or that a loved one is innocent of a criminal charge. In twisted cases, people are self-deceived in believing something that they want to be false (and do not also want to be true). For example, an insecure, jealous husband may believe that his wife is having an affair despite his possessing only relatively flimsy evidence for that proposition and despite his not wanting it to be the case that she is so engaged.[2] If some self-deception is twisted in this sense, at least one relatively common claim about self-deception is false—the claim that *S*'s being self-deceived that *p* requires *S*'s desiring that *p*.[3] Furthermore, twisted self-deception apparently threatens even the more modest claim that all self-deception is motivated or has a motivated component.[4] Although the most obvious antonym of "straight" is "bent," I prefer "twisted" here for stylistic reasons. I am not using the term pejoratively and I do not regard twisted self-deception as essentially pathological.)

In Chapters 2 and 3, I offer an account of the nature and etiology of garden-variety straight self-deception and resolve some familiar puzzles about self-deception. In Chapter 4, I review and reject attempted empirical demonstrations of a "strict" kind of self-deception in which the self-deceiver believes a proposition, *p*, while also believing its negation, ~*p*. In Chapter 5, I develop a pair of approaches to explaining twisted self-deception—a motivation-centered approach and a hybrid approach featuring both motivation and emotion—in order to display our resources for exploring and explaining twisted self-deception and to show that promising approaches are consistent with my position on straight self-deception.

2. Three Approaches to Characterizing Self-Deception and a Pair of Puzzles

In defining self-deception, three common approaches may be distinguished: *lexical*, in which a theorist starts with a definition of "deceive" or "deception," using the dictionary or common usage as a guide, and then employs it as a model for defining self-deception; *example-based*, in which one scrutinizes representative examples of self-deception and attempts to identify their essential common features; and *theory-guided*, in which the search for a definition is guided by commonsense theory about the etiology and nature of self-deception. Hybrids of these approaches are also common.

The lexical approach may seem safest. Practitioners of the example-based approach run the risk of considering too narrow a range of cases. The theory-guided approach, in its typical manifestations, relies on commonsense explanatory hypotheses that may be misguided: even if ordinary folks are good at identifying hypothetical cases of self-deception, they may be quite unreliable at diagnosing what happens in them. In its most pristine versions, the lexical approach relies primarily on a dictionary definition of "deceive." And what could be a better source of definitions than the dictionary?

Matters are not so simple, however. There are weaker and stronger senses of "deceive" both in the dictionary and in common parlance. Lexicalists need a sense of "deceive" that is appropriate to self-deception. On what basis are they to identify that sense? Must they eventually turn to representative examples of self-deception or to commonsense theories about what happens in instances of self-deception?

The lexical approach is favored by theorists who deny that self-deception is possible (e.g., Gergen 1985; Haight 1980; Kipp 1980). A pair of lexical assumptions is common:

1. By definition, person *A* deceives person *B* (where *B* may or may not be the same person as *A*) into believing that *p* only if *A* knows, or at least believes truly, that ~*p* and causes *B* to believe that *p*.
2. By definition, deceiving is an intentional activity: nonintentional deceiving is conceptually impossible.

Each assumption is associated with a familiar puzzle about self-deception.

If assumption 1 is true, then deceiving oneself into believing that *p* requires that one knows, or at least believes truly, that ~*p* and causes oneself to believe that *p*. At the very least, one starts out believing that ~*p* and then somehow gets oneself to believe that *p*. Some theorists take this to entail that, at some time, self-deceivers both believe that *p* and believe that ~*p* (e.g., Kipp 1980, p. 309). And, it is claimed, this is not a possible state of mind: the very nature of belief precludes one's simultaneously believing that *p* is true and believing that *p* is false.[5] Thus we have a *static* puzzle about self-deception: self-deception, according to the view at issue, requires being in an impossible *state of mind*.

In fact, assumption 1 does not entail that in all instances of deceiving, there is some time at which the deceiver believes that ~*p* and the deceived person believes that *p*. In some cases of interpersonal deception, *A* has ceased believing that ~*p* by the time he causes *B* to believe that *p*. Imagine that the vehicle for *A*'s attempted deception is a letter. In his letter, *A* attempts to deceive *B* into believing that *p* by lying to him: *p* is false and his assertion of *p* in the letter is a lie. When he sends the letter, *A* is confident that ~*p*, but he comes to believe that *p* by the time *B* receives the letter. If *A*'s lie is successful, *A* deceives *B* into believing that *p* in a way that provides confirmation for assumption 1. But there is no time at which *A* believes that ~*p* and *B* believes that *p* (see Sorensen 1985).

A theorist inclined to believe that there is a basis in "the concept of deception" for the claim that self-deceivers simultaneously believe that *p* and believe that ~*p* need not be undone by the preceding observation. It may well be true that in *stereotypical* cases of interpersonal deceiving there is some time at which *A* believes that ~*p* and *B* believes that *p*. And it is open to a theorist to contend that self-deception is properly understood only on the model of stereotypical interpersonal deception.

The claim that self-deception must be understood on the model just mentioned produces a further puzzle about the state of self-deception. In stereotypical cases of interpersonal deceiving, there is a time at which the deceiver does *not* have a belief that *p* and the deceived person does have a belief that *p*. If self-deception is strictly analogous to stereotypical interpersonal deception, there is a time at which the self-deceiver both has a belief that *p* and does not have a belief that *p*—a perplexing condition, indeed.[6]

Assumption 2 generates a *dynamic* puzzle, a puzzle about the dynamics of self-deception. On the one hand, it is hard to imagine how one person can deceive another into believing that *p* if the latter person knows exactly what the former is up to, and it is difficult to see how the trick can be any easier when the intending deceiver and the intended victim are the same person. On the other, deception normally is facilitated by the deceiver's having and intentionally executing a deceptive strategy. If, to avoid thwarting one's own efforts at self-deception, one must not intentionally execute any strategy for deceiving oneself, how can one succeed? The challenge is to explain how self-deception in general is a psychologically possible process. If self-deceivers intentionally deceive themselves, one wonders what prevents the guiding intention from undermining its own effective functioning. And if self-deception is not intentional, what motivates and directs processes of self-deception?[7]

A theorist who believes that self-deception is a genuine phenomenon may attempt to solve the puzzles while leaving assumptions 1 and 2 unchallenged. An alternative tack is to undermine these assumptions and to display the relevance of their falsity to a proper understanding of self-deception. That is the line I pursue.

Stereotypical instances of deceiving someone else into believing that *p* are instances of intentional deceiving in which the deceiver knows or believes truly that ~*p*. Recast as claims specifically about *stereotypical* interpersonal deceiving, assumptions 1 and 2 would be acceptable. But in their present formulations the assumptions are false. In a standard use of "deceived" in the passive voice, we properly say such things as "Unless I am deceived, I left my keys in my car." Here "deceived" means "mistaken." There is a corresponding use of "deceive" in the active voice. In this use, to deceive is "to cause to believe what is false," according to the *Oxford English Dictionary.* Obviously, one can intentionally or unintentionally cause someone to believe what is false; and one can cause someone to acquire the false belief that *p* even though one does not oneself believe that ~*p*. Yesterday, mistakenly believing that my daughter's schoolbooks were on my desk, I told her they were there. In so doing, I caused her to believe a falsehood. I deceived her, in the sense identified; but I did not do so intentionally, nor did I cause her to believe something I disbelieved.

The point just made has little significance for self-deception, *if* paradigmatic instances of self-deception have the structure of stereotypical instances of interpersonal deception. But do they? Stock examples of self-deception, both in popular thought and in the literature, feature people who falsely believe—in the face of strong evidence to the contrary—that their spouses are not having affairs, or that their children are not using illicit drugs, or that they themselves are not seriously ill. Is it a plausible diagnosis of what happens in such cases that these people start by knowing or believing the truth, *p*, and intentionally cause themselves to believe that ~*p*? If, in our search for a definition of self-deception, we are guided partly by these stock examples, we may deem it an open question whether self-deception requires intentionally deceiving oneself, getting oneself to believe something one earlier knew or believed to be false, simultaneously possessing conflicting beliefs, and the like. If, instead, our search is driven by a presumption that nothing counts as self-deception unless it has the same structure as stereotypical interpersonal deception, the question is closed at the outset.

Theorists who accept lexical assumptions 1 and 2 may proceed in either of two ways when confronting cases that most people would count as clear instances of self-deception. They may suppose that many such cases are not properly so counted because they fail to satisfy one or both of the assumptions. Alternatively, they may suppose that all or most cases that would generally be deemed clear instances of self-deception do, in fact, satisfy the lexical assumptions, even if they may seem not to. On either alternative, self-deception as a whole is made to seem puzzling. And on the second alternative, as I argue, puzzles are generated in cases that are describable and explicable in quite unpuzzling ways.

Compare the question whether self-deception is properly understood on the model of stereotypical interpersonal deception with the question whether addiction is properly understood on the model of disease. The current folk conception of addiction seemingly treats addictions as being, by definition, diseases. The disease model of addiction, however, has been forcefully attacked (see, e.g., Peele 1989). The issue is essentially about explanation, not about alleged conceptual truths. How is the characteristic behavior of people typically counted as addicts best explained? Is the disease model of addiction explanatorily more accurate or fruitful than its competitors? Self-deception, like addiction, is an explanatory concept. We postulate self-deception in particular cases to explain data: for example, the fact that there are excellent grounds for holding that *S* believes that *p* despite its being the case that evidence *S* possesses makes it quite likely that *~p*. And we should ask how self-deception is likely to be constituted—what it is likely to be—if it does help to explain the relevant data. Should we discover that the data explained by self-deception are *not* explained by a phenomenon involving the simultaneous possession of beliefs whose contents are mutually contradictory or intentional acts of deception directed at oneself, self-deception would not disappear from our conceptual map—any more than addiction would disappear should we learn that addictions are not diseases.

An announcement about belief is in order before I move forward. In the literature on self-deception, belief rather than degree of belief usually is the operative notion. I follow suit in this book, partly to avoid unnecessary complexities. Those who prefer to think in terms of degree of belief should read such expressions as "*S* believes that *p*" as shorthand for "*S* believes that *p* to a degree greater than 0.5 (on a scale from 0 to 1)."[8]

3. Motivationally Biased Belief and Agency

That there are motivationally biased beliefs is difficult to deny. In a passage from which I quoted at the beginning of this chapter, Thomas Gilovich reports:

> A survey of one million high school seniors found that 70% thought they were above average in leadership ability, and only 2% thought they were below average. In terms of ability to get along with others, *all* students thought they were above average, 60% thought they were in the top 10%, and 25% thought they were in the top 1%! . . . A survey of university professors found that 94% thought they were better at their jobs than their average colleague. (1991, p. 77)

If we assume the sincerity of the people surveyed, a likely hypothesis is that motivation had a hand in producing many of the beliefs reported. The aggregated self-assessments are radically out of line with the facts (e.g., only 1 percent can be in the top 1 percent), and the qualities asked about are desirable ones. We may have a tendency to believe propositions that we want to be true even when an impartial investigation of readily available data would indicate that they are probably false. A plausible hypothesis about that tendency is that our desiring something to be true sometimes exerts a biasing influence on what we believe. And there is evidence that our beliefs about our own traits "become more biased when the trait is highly desirable or undesirable" (Brown and Dutton 1995, p. 1290).

Ziva Kunda ably defends the view that motivation can influence "the generation and evaluation of hypotheses, of inference rules, and of evidence," and that motivationally "biased memory search will result in the formation of additional biased beliefs and theories" that cohere with "desired conclusions" (1990, p. 483). In an especially persuasive study, undergraduate subjects (seventy-five women and eighty-six men) read an article alleging that "women were endangered by caffeine and were strongly advised to avoid caffeine in any form"; that the major danger was fibrocystic disease, "associated in its advanced stages with breast cancer"; and that "caffeine induced the disease by increasing the concentration of a substance called cAMP in the breast" (Kunda 1987, p. 642). (Because the article did not personally threaten men, they were used as a control group.) Subjects were then asked to indicate, among other things, "how convinced they were of the connection between caffeine and fibrocystic disease and of the connection between caffeine and . . . cAMP on a 6-point scale" (pp. 643–44). In the female group, "heavy consumers" of caffeine were significantly less convinced of the connections than were "low consumers." The males were considerably more convinced than the female "heavy consumers"; and there was a much smaller difference in conviction between "heavy" and "low" male caffeine consumers (the heavy consumers were slightly *more* convinced of the connections).

Because all subjects were exposed to the same information and arguably only the female "heavy consumers" were personally threatened by it, a plausible hypothesis is that their lower level of conviction is motivated in some way by a desire that their coffee drinking has not significantly endangered their health (cf. Kunda 1987, p. 644). Indeed, in a study in which the reported hazards of caffeine use were relatively modest, "female heavy consumers were no less convinced by the evidence than were female low consumers" (p. 644). Along with the lesser threat, there is less motivation for skepticism about the evidence.

How do the female heavy consumers come to be less convinced than the others? One testable possibility is that because they find the "connections" at issue personally threatening, these women (or some of them) are motivated to take a hypercritical stance toward the article, looking much harder than other subjects for reasons to be skeptical about its merits (cf.

Kunda 1990, p. 495; Liberman and Chaiken 1992). Another is that, owing to the threatening nature of the article, they (or some of them) read it *less* carefully than the others do, thereby enabling themselves to be less impressed by it.[9] In either case, must we suppose that the women intend to deceive themselves, or intend to bring it about that they hold certain beliefs, or start by finding the article convincing and then try to get themselves to find it less convincing? Or can motivation issue in biased beliefs without the assistance of such intentions or efforts?

Consider the following two bold theses about motivationally biased beliefs.

1. The agency view: all motivationally biased beliefs are intentionally produced or protected. In every instance of motivationally biased belief that *p*, we try to bring it about that we acquire or retain the belief that *p*, or at least try to make it easier for ourselves to acquire or retain the belief.
2. The antiagency view: no motivationally biased beliefs are intentionally produced or protected. In no instance of motivationally biased belief that *p* does one try to bring it about that one acquires or retains the belief or try to make it easier for oneself to acquire or retain the belief.

One suspects that the truth lies somewhere between these poles. But which of the two theses is likely to be closer to the truth?

One problem for the agency view is central to the dynamic puzzle about self-deception. The attempts to which the view appeals threaten to undermine themselves. If I am trying to bring it about that I believe that I am a good driver—not by improving my driving skills, but perhaps by ignoring or downplaying evidence that I am an inferior driver while searching for evidence of my having superior driving skills—won't I see that the "grounds" for belief that I arrive at in this way are illegitimate? And won't I therefore find myself still lacking the belief that I am a good driver. A predictable reply is that the "tryings" or efforts to which the agency view appeals are not conscious efforts and therefore need not stand in the way of their own success in the way just envisioned. Whether, and to what extent, we should postulate unconscious tryings in attempting to explain motivationally biased belief depends on what the alternatives are.

The main problem for the antiagency view is also linked to the dynamic puzzle about self-deception. Apparently, we encounter difficulties in trying to understand how motivationally biased beliefs—or many such beliefs—can arise, if not through efforts of the kind the agency view postulates. How, for example, can my wanting it to be the case that I am a good driver motivate me to believe that I am a good driver except by motivating me to try to bring it about that I believe this or by motivating me to try to make it easier for myself to believe this?[10] At the very least, the antiagency view is faced with a clear challenge: to provide an alternative account of the mechanism(s) by which desires lead to motivationally biased beliefs. I take up this challenge in Chapters 2 and 3, in developing a position on the nature and etiology of garden-variety straight self-deception, and I return to it in Chapter 4, in rebutting an alleged empirical demonstration of "strict" self-deception.

Ideally, in exploring the relative merits of the agency and antiagency views, one would start with uncontroversial analyses of *intentional action* and *trying*. Paul Moser and I have offered an analysis of intentional action (Mele and Moser 1994), and Frederick Adams and I have offered an account of trying (Adams and Mele 1992). If I were to deem these offerings uncontroversial, however, the hypothesis that I am merely self-deceived would be quite generous. Fortunately, for the purposes of this book, full-blown analyses of these notions are not required. But some conceptual spade work is in order.

The question how much control an agent must have over an outcome for that outcome to count as *intentionally* produced has elicited strikingly opposed intuitions. According to Christopher Peacocke, it is "undisputed" that an agent who makes a successful attempt "to hit a croquet ball through a distant hoop" *intentionally* hits the ball through the hoop (1985, p. 69). But Brian O'Shaughnessy maintains that a novice who similarly succeeds in hitting the bull's-eye on a dart board does not intentionally hit the bull's-eye (1980, 2:325; cf. Harman 1986, p. 92). This conceptual issue can be skirted, for the purposes of this book, by focusing on whether people who acquire motivationally biased beliefs that *p* *try* to bring it about that they acquire beliefs that *p*, or try to make it easier for themselves to acquire these beliefs. If they do try to do this, one need not worry about whether the success of their attempts owes too much to luck, or to factors beyond the agents' control, for it to be true that they *intentionally* brought it about that they believed that *p*. (Trying to *A*, as I understand it, does not require making a *special* effort to *A*. When I typed the word "special" a moment ago, I was trying to do that, even though I encountered no special resistance and made no remarkable effort to type it.)

Furthermore, if they do *not* try to do this, there is, I believe, no acceptable sense of "intentionally" in which they intentionally bring it about that they believe that *p*. Unfortunately, here one confronts another controversy in the philosophy of action. Some philosophers contend that an agent who tries to do *A*, recognizing that her doing *B* is a likely consequence of her doing *A*, may properly be said to do *B* intentionally (if she does *B*), even if she does not try to do *B* and is in no way attracted to doing *B* (e.g., as a means or as an end), and even if she prefers that her doing *A* not have her doing *B* as a side effect (Bratman 1987, chs. 8–10; Harman 1976). Others reject this idea, contending, roughly, that aside from tryings themselves, we intentionally do only what we try to do (Adams 1986; McCann

1986b, 1991; Mele and Moser 1994; O'Shaughnessy 1980). Steven Sverdlik and I have criticized the grounds for the former view (Mele and Sverdlik 1996), and I do not reopen the debate here. For present purposes, the crucial question is whether motivated beliefs that one is self-deceived in holding are (necessarily, always, or ordinarily) beliefs that one *tries* to bring about or promote. Theorists who favor an affirmative answer often deem the trying involved—or the associated intentions—to be unconscious (Bermudez 1997; Martin 1997; Talbott 1995, 1997), and I assume, accordingly, that unconscious tryings and intentions are possible.

Intentionally deceiving oneself is unproblematically possible. It is worth noting, however, that the unproblematic cases are remote from garden-variety self-deception. Here is an illustration. Ike, a forgetful prankster skilled at imitating others' handwriting, has intentionally deceived friends by secretly making false entries in their diaries. Ike has just decided to deceive himself by making a false entry in his own diary. Cognizant of his forgetfulness, he writes under today's date, "I was particularly brilliant in class today," counting on eventually forgetting that what he wrote is false. Weeks later, when reviewing his diary, Ike reads this sentence and acquires the belief that he was brilliant in class on the specified day. If Ike intentionally deceived others by making false entries in their diaries, what is to prevent us from justifiably holding that he intentionally deceived himself in the imagined case? He intended to bring it about that he would believe that *p*, which he knew at the time to be false; and he executed that intention without a hitch, causing himself to believe, eventually, that *p*. Again, to deceive, on one standard definition, is to cause to believe what is false; and Ike's causing himself to believe the relevant falsehood is no less intentional than his causing his friends to believe falsehoods (by doctoring their diaries).[11]

Ike's case undoubtedly strikes readers as markedly dissimilar to garden-variety examples of self-deception—for instance, the case of the woman who falsely believes that her child is not using drugs (or that she is healthy or that her husband is not having an affair), in the face of strong evidence to the contrary. Why is that? The most obvious difference between Ike's case and garden-variety examples of self-deception lies in the straightforwardly intentional nature of Ike's project. Ike consciously sets out to deceive himself and he intentionally and consciously executes his plan for so doing; ordinary self-deceivers behave quite differently.[12]

This suggests that in attempting to construct hypothetical cases that are, at once, paradigmatic cases of self-deception and cases of agents intentionally deceiving themselves, one should imagine that the agents' intentions to deceive themselves are somehow hidden from them. I do not wish to claim that "hidden intentions" are impossible. Our ordinary concept of intention may leave room, for example, for "Freudian" intentions, hidden in some mental partition. And if there is conceptual space for hidden intentions that play a role in the etiology of behavior, there is conceptual space for hidden intentions to deceive ourselves, intentions that may influence our treatment of data. As I see it, the claim is *unwarranted*, *not* incoherent, that intentions to deceive ourselves, or intentions to produce or sustain certain beliefs in ourselves, or corresponding attempts—normally, intentions or attempts hidden from us—are at work in ordinary self-deception.[13] Without denying that "hidden intention" or "hidden attempt" cases of self-deception are possible, a theorist should ask what evidence there may be (in the real world) that intentions or attempts to deceive oneself, or to make it easier for oneself to believe something, are at work in garden-variety self-deception. Are there data that can *only*—or *best*—be explained on the hypothesis that such intentions or attempts are operative in such self-deception? The answer that I defend in subsequent chapters is *no*.

Distinguishing activities of the following three kinds will prove useful. Regarding cognitive activities that contribute to motivationally biased belief, there are significant differences among (1) *unintentional* activities (e.g., unintentionally focusing on data of a certain kind), (2) *intentional* activities (e.g., intentionally focusing on data of a certain kind), and (3) intentional activities engaged in as part of an *attempt* to deceive oneself, or to cause oneself to believe something, or to make it easier for oneself to believe something (e.g., intentionally focusing on data of a certain kind as part of an attempt to deceive oneself into believing that *p*). Many skeptical worries about the reality of self-deception are motivated partly by the assumption that activity of the third kind is characteristic of self-deception.

An important difference between the second and third kinds of activity merits emphasis. Imagine a twelve-year-old, Beth, whose father died some months ago. Beth may find it comforting to reflect on pleasant memories of playing happily with her father, to look at family photographs of such scenes, and the like. Similarly, she may find it unpleasant to reflect on memories of her father leaving her behind to play ball with her brothers, as he frequently did. From time to time, she may intentionally focus her attention on the pleasant memories, intentionally linger over the pictures, and intentionally turn her attention away from memories of being left behind and from pictures of her father playing only with her brothers. As a consequence of such intentional activities, she may acquire a false, unwarranted belief that her father cared more deeply for her than for anyone else. Although her intentional cognitive activities may be explained, in part, by the motivational attractiveness of the hypothesis that he loved her most, those activities need not also be explained by a desire—much less an intention or an attempt—to deceive herself into believing this hypothesis, or to cause herself to believe this, or to make it easier for herself to believe this. Intentional cognitive activities that contribute even in a relatively straightforward way to motivationally biased, false, unwarranted belief need not be guided by an intention of any of the kinds just mentioned, nor need they involve associated attempts to manipulate what one believes. Beth's activities are explicable on the hypothesis that she was seeking pleasant experiences and avoiding painful ones without in any way trying to influence what she believed. Whether a case like the present one is plausibly counted as an instance of self-deception remains to be seen.

Obviously, an agent's doing something that he is trying to do can have a result that he does not try to produce. Intending to turn on a light in an unfamiliar kitchen, Al tries to flip the switch on his left, and he succeeds in flipping it. As it happens, that switch is wired to the garbage disposal. So Al turns on the garbage disposal, but he does not try to do that. Similarly, Beth tries to focus her attention on certain memories and photographs and tries to avoid focusing it on certain other things, and she succeeds in this. Perhaps, in doing these things, she is also trying to comfort herself. Beth's cognitive activities result in her believing that her father loved her most. But, clearly, these points do not entail that Beth is trying to produce this belief or trying to make it easier for herself to acquire this belief—any more than similar points about Al entail that he is trying to activate the garbage disposal.

Another illustration of the difference between the second and third kinds of activity may prove useful. Donald Gorassini has suggested that an intentional form of self-deception is quite common (1997, p. 116). Described in a theory-neutral way, what Gorassini has in mind are cases in which a person who lacks a certain quality—for example, kindness—but is desirous of its being true that he has that quality is motivated to act *as if* he has it and then infers from his behavior that he does have it. I discussed cases of this kind previously under the rubric "acting as if" (Mele 1987a, pp. 151–58). One of the points I made is that an agent's motivation to act as if *p* may have sources of various kinds. Here are two examples. Ann believes that she can cultivate the trait of kindness in herself by acting as if she were kind; so, because she wants to become kind, she decides to embark on a program of acting as if she were kind, and she acts accordingly. Because Bob would like to be a generous person, he finds pleasure in actions of his that are associated with the trait; consequently, Bob has hedonic motivation to act as if he were generous, and he sometimes acts accordingly. Unlike Ann, Bob is not trying to inculcate the desired trait in himself.

There is considerable evidence that we often make inferences about our qualities on the basis of our own behavior (see, e.g., Bem 1972). It is easy to imagine that, after some time, Ann and Bob infer, largely from their relevant behavior, that they have the desired trait, even though they in fact lack it. However, from the facts that these agents want it to be true that *p*, intentionally act as if *p* owing significantly to their wanting *p* to be true, and come to believe that *p* largely as a consequence of that intentional behavior, it does not follow that they were trying to deceive themselves into believing that *p* or trying to make it easier for themselves to believe that *p*. Ann may simply have been trying to make herself kind and Bob may merely have been seeking the pleasure that acts associated with generosity give him.

A related point may be made about cases in which one's desire that *p* and intentional behavior that it motivates lead to biased beliefs about one's traits via a route that has a major social component. An older boy who is strongly desirous of its being true that he is a natural leader but who lacks the admiration of his peers may find the company of younger, impressionable teenagers considerably more pleasant. His hedonically motivated choice of younger companions may result in selective exposure to data supportive of the hypothesis that he is a natural leader; the younger teenagers might worship him. This choice and the social feedback it helps generate may contribute significantly to his acquiring an unwarranted, biased belief about his leadership ability. But to explain what happens in such a case, there is no need to suppose that the boy was trying to get himself to believe that he was a natural leader, or trying to make it easier for himself to believe this.

The following remarks by David Pears and Donald Davidson on the self-deceptive acquisition of a motivationally biased belief are concise expressions of two different "agency" views of the phenomenon:

> [There is a] sub-system . . . built around the nucleus of the wish for the irrational belief and it is organized like a person. Although it is a separate centre of agency within the whole person, it is, from its own point of view, entirely rational. It wants the main system to form the irrational belief and it is aware that it will not form it, if the cautionary belief [i.e., the belief that it would be irrational to form the desired belief] is allowed to intervene. So with perfect rationality it stops its intervention. (Pears 1984, p. 87)

> His practical reasoning is straightforward. Other things being equal, it is better to avoid pain; believing he will fail the exam is painful; therefore (other things being equal) it is better to avoid believing he will fail the exam. Since it is a condition of his problem that he take the exam, this means it would be better to believe he will pass. He does things to promote this belief. (Davidson 1985, pp. 145–46)

Both views rest largely on the thought that the only way, or the best way, to account for certain data is to hold that the person, or some center of agency within the person, tries to bring it about that the person, or some "system" in the person, holds a certain belief. In subsequent chapters, I argue that we can account for the pertinent data in more plausible and less problematic ways.

Consider a case of self-deception similar to the one Davidson diagnoses in the passage just quoted. Carlos "has good reason to believe" that he will fail his driver's test (p. 145). "He has failed the test twice before and his instructor has said discouraging things. On the other hand, he knows the examiner personally, and he has faith in his own charm" (pp. 145–46). "The thought of failing the test once again is painful to Carlos (in fact the thought of failing anything is particularly galling to Carlos)." Suppose that the overwhelming majority of Carlos's impartial cognitive peers presented with his evidence would believe that Carlos will fail the test and that none of them would believe that Carlos will pass it. (Perhaps some peers with particularly high standards for belief would withhold belief.) Even so, in the face of the evidence to the contrary, Carlos believes that he will pass. Predictably, he fails.

If lexical assumption 1 about deception were true (see sec. 2), then, on the assumption that Carlos is self-deceived in believing that he will pass the test, he believed at some time that he would fail the test. In accommodating the data offered in my description of the case, however, there is no evident need to suppose that Carlos had this true belief. Perhaps his self-deception is such that not only does he acquire the belief that he will pass the test, but he never acquires the belief that he will fail. In fact, at least at first sight, it seems that this is true of much self-deception. Seemingly, at least some parents who are self-deceived in believing that their children have never experimented with drugs and some people who are self-deceived in believing that their spouses have not had affairs have at no point believed that these things have happened. Owing to self-deception, they have not come to believe the truth, and perhaps they never will.

That having been said, it does seem that there are cases in which a person who once believed an unpleasant truth, *p*, later is self-deceived in believing that ~*p*. For example, a mother who once believed that her son was using drugs subsequently comes to believe that he has never used drugs and is self-deceived in so believing. Does a change of mind of this sort *require* an exercise of agency of the kind postulated by Pears or Davidson?

Is such a change of mind *most plausibly explained*, at least, on the hypothesis that an exercise of agency of one of these kinds occurred? A theorist who attends to the stark descriptions Pears and Davidson offer of the place of agency in self-deception should at least wonder whether things are in fact so straightforward.

It is often supposed that, as one philosopher has put it, (1) "desires have no explanatory force without associated beliefs" that identify means, or apparent means, to the desires' satisfaction and (2) this is part of "the very logic of belief-desire explanation" (Foss 1997, p. 112). Setting aside intentional *A*-ings that are motivated by intrinsic desires to *A* (i.e., desires that treat one's *A*-ing as an end), claim 1 may be part of the logic of belief-desire explanation of *intentional action*.[14] But the claim does not fare well in the sphere or motivationally biased belief.

Recall the "survey of one million high school seniors" that found, among other things, that "25% thought they were in the top 1%" in ability to get along with others (Gilovich 1991, p. 77). The figures are striking, and a likely hypothesis about them includes the idea that desires that *p* can contribute to biased beliefs that *p*. If claim 1 were true, a student's wanting it to be the case that she has superior ability to get along with others would help to explain her believing that she is superior in this area only in conjunction with some instrumental belief that links her believing that she is superior in this area to the satisfaction of her desire to be superior. But one searches in vain for instrumental beliefs that would both turn the trick and be plausibly widely attributed to high school seniors. Perhaps believing that one has a superior ability to get along with others can help to bring it about that one is in fact superior in this sphere, and some high school students might believe that this is so. But it is highly unlikely that most people who have a motivationally biased belief that they have a superior ability to get along with others have this belief, in part, *because* they want it to be true that they are superior in this area *and* believe that believing that they are superior can make it so. And no other instrumental belief looks more promising.

Should we infer, then, that wanting it to be the case that one has a superior ability to get along with others plays a role in explaining only relatively few instances of false and unwarranted belief that one is superior in this area? Not at all. There is powerful empirical evidence, some of which is reviewed in Chapter 2, that desiring that *p* makes a broad causal contribution to the acquisition and retention of unwarranted beliefs that *p*. Desires that do this properly enter into causal *explanations* of the pertinent biased beliefs. It is a mistake to assume that the role characteristic of desires in explaining intentional actions is the only explanatory role desires can have.

If Pears or Davidson is right about a case like the mother's or Carlos's, presumably similar exercises of agency are at work in an enormous number of high school students who believe that, regarding ability to get along with others, they are "in the top 1%" and in a great many university professors who believe that they are better at what they do than their average colleague. Perhaps self-deception is very common, but the same is unlikely to be true of intentional self-manipulation of the kind Pears or Davidson describes. Theorists inclined to agree with claims 1 and 2 about the explanatory force of desires will be inclined toward some version of the agency view of motivationally biased belief and self-deception. As I will argue, however, desires contribute to the production of motivationally biased beliefs, including beliefs that one is self-deceived in holding, in a variety of relatively well understood ways that fit the anti-agency model.

2

Garden-Variety Straight Self-Deception: Some Psychological Processes

As I pointed out in Chapter 1, standard examples of self-deception feature people who falsely believe—in the face of strong evidence to the contrary—things that they would like to be true: for example, that their children are not using illicit drugs, or that they themselves are healthy. Garden-variety straight self-deception is commonly regarded as a *motivated* phenomenon. Should it turn out that it is motivated in a way that ensures that self-deceivers start by believing that *~p* and try to deceive themselves into believing that *p*, theorists who seek a tight fit between self-deception and stereotypical interpersonal deception would be vindicated. As I argue here and in the next two chapters, however, it is likely that what happens in garden-variety straight self-deception is consistent with the antiagency view and is both more subtle and less problematic than interpersonal models imply. My focus in the present chapter is a collection of processes that contribute to motivationally biased beliefs, including beliefs that people are self-deceived in acquiring.

1. Desires and Biases

Our desiring that *p* can contribute in a variety of ways to our believing that *p* in instances of straight self-deception. I offer four examples.[1]

1. *Negative misinterpretation.* Our desiring that *p* may lead us to misinterpret as not counting (or not counting strongly) against *p* data that we would easily recognize to count (or count strongly) against *p* in the desire's absence. For example, Don just received a rejection notice on a journal submission. He hopes that his article was *wrongly* rejected, and he reads through the comments offered. Don decides that the referees misunderstood a certain crucial but complex point and that their objections consequently do not justify the rejection. As it turns out, however, the referees' criticisms were entirely justified, and a few days later, when Don rereads his paper and the comments in a more impartial frame of mind, it is clear to him that the rejection was warranted.

2. *Positive misinterpretation.* Our desiring that *p* may lead us to interpret as *supporting p* data that we would easily recognize to count against *p* in the desire's absence. For example, Sid is very fond of Roz, a college classmate with whom he often studies. Wanting it to be true that Roz loves him, he may interpret her refusing to date him and her reminding him that she has a steady boyfriend as an effort on her part to "play hard to get" in order to encourage Sid to continue to pursue her and prove that his love for her approximates hers for him. As Sid interprets Roz's behavior, not only does it fail to count against the hypothesis that she loves him, it is evidence *for* the truth of that hypothesis.

3. *Selective focusing/attending.* Our desiring that *p* may lead us both to fail to focus attention on evidence that counts against *p* and to focus instead on evidence suggestive of *p*. Recall the example of Beth, the child whose father died prematurely (ch. 1, sec. 3). Owing partly to her desire that she was her father's favorite, she finds it comforting to attend to memories and photographs that place her in the spotlight of her father's affection and unpleasant to attend to memories and photographs that

place a sibling in that spotlight. Accordingly, she focuses her attention on the former and is inattentive to the latter.

4. *Selective evidence-gathering*. Our desiring that *p* may lead us both to overlook easily obtainable evidence for ~*p* and to find evidence for *p* that is much less accessible. For example, Betty, a political campaign staffer who thinks the world of her candidate, has heard rumors from the opposition that he is sexist, but she hopes that he is not. That hope motivates her to scour his past voting record for evidence of his political correctness on gender issues and to consult people in her own campaign office about his personal behavior. Betty may miss rather obvious and weighty evidence that her boss is sexist—which he in fact is—even though she succeeds in finding less obvious and less weighty evidence for her favored view. Selective evidence-gathering may be analyzed as a combination of hypersensitivity to evidence (and sources of evidence) for the desired state of affairs and blindness—of which there are, of course, degrees—to contrary evidence (and sources thereof).[2]

In none of these examples does the person hold the true belief that ~*p* and then intentionally bring it about that he or she believes that *p*. Yet, if we assume that my hypothetical agents acquire relevant false, unwarranted beliefs in the ways described, these are garden-variety instances of self-deception.[3] Don is self-deceived in believing that his article was wrongly rejected, Sid is self-deceived in believing certain things about Roz, and so on.

We have at least an intuitive grip on how a desire that *p* can trigger and sustain each of the four processes that I have just described and lead to a biased belief that *p*. That grip is strongest in the case of selective focusing or attending. We can understand why, owing to her desire that her father loved her most, Beth finds it pleasant to attend to photographs and memories featuring her as the object of her father's affection and painful to attend to photographs and memories that put others in the place she prizes. We also recognize that people tend to seek pleasure and to avoid pain and that some attentional activities are quite pleasant or painful. Furthermore, we have at least an intuitive understanding of how selectively attending to evidence for *p* can increase the probability that one will acquire a belief that *p*. But how do desires that *p* trigger and sustain the two kinds of misinterpretation and selective evidence-gathering, thereby leading to biased beliefs that *p*? It is not as though these activities are intrinsically pleasant, as attending to pleasant memories, for example, is intrinsically pleasant. The answer lies elsewhere.

Beliefs that we are self-deceived in acquiring or retaining are a species of *biased* belief. In self-deception, on a widely held view, the biasing is *motivated*. Even so, attention to some potential sources of *unmotivated* or "cold" biased belief is instructive. I offer three such sources that have been identified in the psychological literature.

1. *Vividness of information*. A datum's vividness for an individual often is a function of individual interests, the concreteness of the datum, its "imagery-provoking" power, or its sensory, temporal, or spatial proximity (Nisbett and Ross 1980, p. 45). Vivid data are more likely to be recognized, attended to, and recalled than pallid data. Consequently, vivid data tend to have a disproportional influence on the formation and retention of beliefs.[4]

2. *The availability heuristic*. When we form beliefs about the frequency, likelihood, or causes of an event, we "often may be influenced by the relative availability of the objects or events, that is, their accessibility in the processes of perception, memory, or construction from imagination" (Nisbett and Ross 1980, p. 18). For example, we may mistakenly believe that the number of English words beginning with *r* greatly outstrips the number having *r* in the third position, because we find it much easier

to produce words on the basis of a search for their first letter (Tversky and Kahnemann 1973). Similarly, attempts to locate the cause(s) of an event are significantly influenced by manipulations that focus one's attention on a specific potential cause (Nisbett and Ross 1980, p. 22; Taylor and Fiske 1975, 1978).

3. *The confirmation bias.* People testing a hypothesis tend to search (in memory and the world) more often for confirming than for disconfirming instances and to recognize the former more readily (Baron 1988, pp. 259–65; Klayman and Ha 1987; Nisbett and Ross 1980, pp. 181–82), even when the hypothesis is only tentative (as opposed, e.g., to a belief one has). The phenomenon has been observed in the interpretation of relatively neutral data as well. For example, "subjects who tested the hypothesis that a person was angry interpreted that person's facial expression as conveying anger, whereas subjects who tested the hypothesis that the person was happy interpreted the same facial expression as conveying happiness" (Trope, Gervey, and Liberman 1997, p. 115). The implications of the confirmation bias for the retention and formation of beliefs are obvious.

Obviously, the most vivid or available data sometimes have the greatest evidential value; the influence of such data is not *always* a biasing influence. The main point to be made is that, although sources of biased belief can function independently of motivation, they may also be triggered and sustained by motivation in the production of particular *motivationally* biased beliefs.[5] For example, motivation can increase the vividness or salience of certain data. Data that count in favor of the truth of a hypothesis that one would like to be true might be rendered more vivid or salient given one's recognition that they so count; and vivid or salient data, given that they are more likely to be recognized and recalled, tend to be more "available" than pallid counterparts. Similarly, motivation can influence which hypotheses occur to one and affect the salience of available hypotheses, thereby setting the stage for the confirmation bias.[6] Because favorable hypotheses are more pleasant to contemplate than unfavorable ones and tend to come more readily to mind, desiring that *p* increases the probability that one's hypothesis testing will be focused on *p* rather than ~*p* (Trope and Liberman 1996, p. 258; Trope et al. 1997, p. 113). Motivation that triggers and sustains the confirmation bias promotes cognitive behavior that epistemologists shun. In at least some stock examples of self-deception, the false beliefs acquired in the face of weightier evidence to the contrary may be produced or sustained by motivated phenomena of the kinds described. And the self-deception, in these cases, in no way requires that the agents intend or try to deceive themselves, or intend or try to produce or sustain certain beliefs in themselves, or start by believing something they end up disbelieving. Cold biasing obviously is not intentional; and, in particular cases, the functioning of mechanisms of the sort described may be primed and sustained by motivation independently of any intention or attempt to deceive.

My mention of the motivational *sustaining* of the functioning of these mechanisms requires a brief explanation. A fleeting desire that momentarily increases the vividness or availability of a datum, or suggests a fleeting hypothesis, will not, other things being equal, have nearly as strong an effect on belief acquisition as a desire of significantly greater duration. Sid, who is desirous of its being true that Roz is romantically attracted to him, may find evidence of this attraction particularly vivid and available—as long as the desire persists. Over time, owing partly to these features of the evidence, he may come to believe that she loves him. Were he to lose the relevant desire after a few moments (perhaps because he suddenly falls head over heels for Rachel), we would expect a decrease in the vividness and availability of the evidence in question about Roz and, other things being equal, a corresponding decrease in the likelihood that he will acquire the belief at issue.

It is no mystery how the confirmation bias, the availability heuristic, and vividness of information can contribute to the two kinds of misinterpretation and the two kinds of selectivity that I identified. Predictable effects of motivation on the confirmation bias increase the likelihood of biased interpretation and of selective attending and evidence-gathering. The same is true of the effects of motivation on the availability and vividness of data. But there is much more to the story of motivationally biased belief, as I begin to explain in the following section.

2. A Model of Everyday Hypothesis Testing

Some useful recent models of everyday hypothesis testing are designed to accommodate evidence of motivationally biased belief. James Friedrich's "primary error detection and minimization" (PEDMIN) analysis of "lay hypothesis testing" is one such model (1993). Friedrich argues that "detection and minimization of crucial errors is in fact the central organizing principle in lay hypothesis testing" (p. 299). People are "pragmatic reasoners more concerned with minimizing crucial errors or mistakes than with testing for truth" (p. 304). A similar model has been advocated by Yaacov Trope and Akiva Liberman (1996). For reasons of economy, I combine their central ideas into the Friedrich-Trope-Liberman (FTL) model.

On Friedrich's view, lay hypothesis testers proceed as they do partly because they *want* to avoid or minimize "costly errors" (1993, p. 300). This is not to say, however, that in testing hypotheses as they are, lay hypothesis testers normally are consciously aiming at minimizing certain errors, or even unconsciously trying to minimize those errors. Friedrich writes: "Although a PEDMIN analysis is in some respects a type of 'expected value of information' model of hypothesis testing, it does not presume that such computations generally take place in a kind of conscious, thoughtful manner. Strategies may, in fact, be rather automatic and inflexible, once a problem is framed and particular errors become salient, perhaps reflecting the operation of evolved cognitive adaptations to a range of biologically significant problems" (p. 317). "Evolutionary selection pressures may well have favored the development of automatic test strategies that are set in motion once a significant harm or potential error is made salient and primary" (p. 313). Compare this comment with my discussion of motivationally triggered and sustained cold biasing mechanisms.

Further consideration of the confirmation bias proves useful in this connection. Given the tendency that this bias constitutes, a desire that *p*—for example, that one's child is not experimenting with drugs—may, depending on one's other desires at the time and the quality of one's evidence, promote the acquisition or retention of a biased belief that *p* by leading one to test the hypothesis that *p*, as opposed to the hypothesis that ~*p*, and sustaining such a test. The desire's role in the production of the biased belief is its prompting and sustaining a test of a specific hypothesis. With the hypothesis in place that one's child is not experimenting with drugs, one will be more likely to search for, recognize, and attend to evidence for this hypothesis than evidence against it, and more likely, as well, to interpret relatively neutral data as supporting the hypothesis than as challenging it. This obviously will increase the probability that one will come (or continue) to believe that one's child is innocent of drug use. And although the process is triggered and sustained by the desire that one's child is not using drugs, there is no need to suppose that what happens is part of an attempt to bring it about that one believes that one's child is innocent of drug use, or an effort to increase the probability that one will believe this, or an effort to decrease the probability that one will (falsely) believe that one's child is guilty. Rather, on a view like Friedrich's, motivation, in a case like this, triggers and sustains the operation of a habit that in itself is purely cognitive.

Sometimes we generate our own hypotheses, and sometimes hypotheses—including very unpleasant ones—are suggested to us by others. If people were consistently to concentrate primarily on confirmatory instances of hypotheses they are testing, independently of what is at stake, that would indicate that the effect of motivation on hypothesis testing is limited to the role it plays in influencing which hypotheses we (primarily) test and that motivation never plays a separate role in influencing the proportion of attention we give to evidence for the falsity of a hypothesis. However, Friedrich marshals evidence that the "confirmation bias" is considerably less rigid than this. For example, in one study (Gigerenzer and Hug 1992) two groups of subjects are asked to test "social-contract rules such as 'If someone stays overnight in the cabin, then that person must bring along a bundle of firewood' " (Friedrich 1993, p. 313). The group asked to adopt "the perspective of a cabin guard monitoring compliance" showed an "extremely high frequency" of testing for disconfirming instances (i.e., for people who stay in the cabin overnight but bring no wood). The other group, asked to "take the perspective of a visitor trying to determine" whether firewood was supplied by visitors themselves or by a local club, showed the common confirmation bias. Such flexibility or variability in testing strategies is a mark of susceptibility to motivational influence (see Mele 1995, pp. 35–36). This influence on lay hypothesis testing is not a matter of motivation prompting efforts to come to particular conclusions. Nor, on the PEDMIN view as I interpret it, are hypothesis testers guided by an intention to minimize crucial errors rather than to determine whether the hypothesis is true or false. Instead, the influence of motivation on them is such that they tend to test hypotheses for truth and falsity in ways that minimize such errors. For example, the subjects taking the perspective of a cabin guard are testing the conditional assertion for accuracy by looking for violators, which will tend to decrease one relevant kind of error.

One application of the PEDMIN analysis to self-deception is straightforward, and Friedrich himself articulates it. He suggests that, in testing hypotheses that have a bearing on one's self-esteem or self-image,

> a prime candidate for primary error of concern is believing as true something that leads [one] to mistakenly criticize [oneself] or lower [one's] self-esteem. Such costs are generally highly salient and are paid for immediately in terms of psychological discomfort. When there are few costs associated with errors of self-deception (incorrectly preserving or enhancing one's self-image), mistakenly revising one's self-image downward or failing to boost it appropriately should be the focal error. (1993, p. 314)

"Self-deception might . . . occur out of a . . . method of testing that reflects a reasonable lack of concern for errors associated with giving oneself the benefit of the doubt" (1993, p. 314).

Trope and Liberman (1996) offer a relatively precise account of the costs relevant to hypothesis testing in constructing a model of everyday reasoning that resembles Friedrich's PEDMIN model. A central element of Trope and Liberman's model is the notion of a "confidence threshold," or a "threshold," for short. The lower the threshold, the thinner the evidence required to reach it. Two thresholds are relevant to each hypothesis: "The acceptance threshold is the minimum confidence in the truth of a hypothesis that [one] requires before accepting it, rather than continuing to test it, and the rejection threshold is the minimum confidence in the untruth of a hypothesis that [one] requires before rejecting it and discontinuing the test" (p. 253). Trope and Liberman contend that the two thresholds often are not equally demanding and that the acceptance and rejection thresholds respectively depend "primarily" on "the cost of false acceptance relative to the cost of information" and "the cost of false rejection relative to the cost of information" (p. 253).

The various relevant costs are understood as follows. The "cost of information" is simply the "resources and effort" required for acquiring and processing "hypothesis-relevant information" (p. 252). The cost of false acceptance of a hypothesis *p* is a measure of the subjective importance to the individual of avoiding falsely believing that *p*.[7] And the cost of false rejection of the same hypothesis seems similarly to be a measure of the subjective importance of avoiding falsely believing that ~*p*.[8]

Obviously, the actual cost of an event or state may diverge widely from the cost that may reasonably be expected, should that event occur or that state obtain. The actual cost of someone's falsely believing that *p* may be quite surprising: a maniac may secretly stalk and kill people who believe (falsely, of course) that West Virginia is in the western United States. This is not the notion of cost that Friedrich or Trope and Liberman have in mind regarding "inferential errors." Rather, the costs of false acceptance and false rejection of a hypothesis, as I understand these authors, are the costs (including missed opportunities for gains) that it would be reasonable for an agent to expect them to have, given the agent's desires and beliefs, if the agent were to have expectations about such things. This point having been made, I am content to use Trope and Liberman's term, "cost."[9]

A survey that I mentioned in Chapter 1 provides a basis for a simple example of divergent costs, in the pertinent sense, for false acceptance and false rejection of a hypothesis. It is plausible that for most people who want it to be the case that they are above average in leadership ability (or more congenial than the average person, or better at their job than their average colleague), the cost of falsely believing that they are not above average is considerably higher than the cost of falsely believing that they are above average. They would at least pay a relatively immediate and significant hedonic price for acquiring the belief that they lack the property at issue (whether the belief is false or true), and their acquiring the false belief that they have this property would normally be quite harmless. Notice that if

Trope and Liberman are right, then, other things being equal, these people will have a significantly lower threshold for accepting the proposition at issue than for rejecting it.

The FTL model adopts a "pragmatic perspective" according to which "hypothesis testing is motivated by the cost of inferential errors (false acceptance or rejection of a hypothesis) relative to the cost of information" (Trope and Liberman 1996, p. 240)—or motivated, more precisely, by aversions to these costs. "[D]esirable and undesirable hypotheses often produce asymmetric error costs" (p. 240). The sum of the costs for an individual of falsely accepting and of falsely rejecting a hypothesis *p* "represents the hypothesis tester's overall motivation" regarding the testing of *p* (p. 252). Setting aside the cost of information, "high overall motivation may lead" people to consider and test both desirable hypotheses and alternative hypotheses (Trope and Liberman, p. 240; cf. Trope et al. 1997, p. 116). Even so, asymmetric costs, or asymmetric aversions to the pertinent costs, "will bias hypothesis testing by motivating [people] to be more vigilant in avoiding the costlier error" (Trope and Liberman, p. 240; cf. Friedrich 1993). Moreover, error costs also "affect hypothesis testing . . . by determining the extremity of acceptance and rejection thresholds" (Trope and Liberman, p. 264), and if the thresholds for acceptance and rejection of a hypothesis are not the same, the individual will reach "one conclusion more easily than" the other (p. 252).

Obviously, the costs of rejecting a true hypothesis and of accepting a false one are costs relative to the individual's own *motivational* condition. For the parents who fervently hope that their son has been wrongly accused of treason, the cost of rejecting the true hypothesis that he is innocent (considerable emotional distress) may be much higher than the cost of accepting the false hypothesis that he is innocent. For their son's staff of intelligence agents in the CIA, however, the cost of accepting the false hypothesis that he is innocent (considerable personal risk) may be much greater than the cost of rejecting the true hypothesis that he is innocent—even if they would like it to be true that he is innocent. Again, the lower the threshold, the thinner the evidence required to reach it. So, if Trope and Liberman are right, simply by influencing acceptance and rejection thresholds, desires sometimes influence what we come to believe. Moreover, to the extent that desire-shaped error costs influence *how* we test hypotheses, they influence what we come to believe. I return to both points shortly.

Trope and Liberman, following Kruglanski 1989, divide "the hypothesis-testing process" in two: the "generation of a hypothesis and its evaluation" (1996, p. 240). The *generation* of a hypothesis that one will proceed to test is just a matter of that hypothesis's coming to mind. The *evaluation* of a hypothesis includes coming to have a sense of its implications, information gathering, "interpretation or categorization" of the evidence gathered, and making inferences about the truth or falsity of the hypothesis on the basis of the interpreted evidence (pp. 240-41). Desires may bias the process on either side of the divide.

Another illustration of motivationally biased evaluation should prove useful. Bob wants it to be true that he is the best third baseman in his league. Owing partly to that desire, he has a lower threshold for believing that he is than for believing that he is not. Bob examines the statistics on the competition and decides, correctly, that his main competitor is Carl. Bob and Carl have the same fielding percentage, but Carl has a few more home runs (28 vs. 25), several more runs batted in (70 vs. 62), and a higher batting average (.370 vs. .345). However, Carl's team is much better than Bob's, and, as Bob knows, players on better teams tend to have more opportunities to bat in runs (because teammates tend to be on base more often) and to hit home runs (because, in various situations, pitchers will walk excellent hitters to pitch to a weak hitter). Bob takes all this and more into account and comes to believe that he is a better player than Carl. As it turns out, however, a panel of experts properly decides that Carl is the better player, and they select Bob as the backup third baseman for the all-star team. They too take account of the fact that Carl's team was far superior to Bob's, but they also notice that Carl batted many fewer times than Bob (250 vs. 320). (Carl's coach often rested him against weak teams.) And they are impressed that, given this statistic, Carl still outperformed Bob in home runs and runs batted in.

On the FTL model, Bob's coming to the conclusion he does is explained in significant part by his having a lower threshold for believing that he is better than Carl than for believing that this is not so, and this in turn is largely explained by his wanting it to be the case that he is the better player. Given the difference in thresholds, Bob's acquiring the belief that he is the better player requires less evidential support than does his acquiring the belief that this is not the case. Perhaps Bob's recognition that his statistics are almost as good as Carl's, in conjunction with his observation that players on better teams tend to have more opportunities for runs batted in and home runs, is enough to bring Bob across the threshold for belief that he is the better player. Having made it there, he might not even stop to think about the implications of Carl's having batted many fewer times.

Bob's belief that he is a better player than Carl certainly seems to be a motivationally biased one. And there is no evident need to suppose that Bob tried to bring it about that he believed, or tried to make it easier for himself to believe, that he is the better player, or tried to reduce the probability that he would believe that Carl is the better player. His coming to the belief he did can be accommodated by the FTL model without supposing that he engaged in such exercises of agency.

For my purposes in this book, there is no need to embrace the FTL model of lay hypothesis testing in its full generality. This is fortunate, because there are grounds for caution about the model. If, as Friedrich claims, "lay hypothesis testers . . . are always directionally motivated in that they are concerned with particular errors to the relative neglect of others" (1993, p. 300),[10] instances of the confirmation bias are *uniformly* to be explained at least partially in terms of PEDMIN motivation—motivation to minimize crucial errors. But it is consistent with the data he discusses that, for example, disproportionate attention to *A*s, or to *A*s that are *B*s, when testing hypotheses of the form "More *A*s than non-*A*s are *B*s" often is an unmotivated manifestation of a purely cognitive habit and that logically appropriate attention to non-*A*s in lay hypothesis testers is explained by PEDMIN motivation (or, sometimes, by the unmotivated salience of certain possible errors).[11] The confirmation bias regarding sentences of this form might often manifest a cognitive *default* mechanism or habit that is neither triggered nor sustained by motivation; PEDMIN motivation might override the default mechanism in cases in which it is important to the individual to detect a false hypothesis.[12]

Although Friedrich acknowledges that the reasoning of lay hypothesis testers sometimes accords with canonical scientific or logical procedure, he contends that this is probably a "byproduct" of PEDMIN motivation (p. 313).[13] Now, regarding many propositions *p*, one may be indifferent between avoiding falsely believing that *p* is true and avoiding falsely believing that *p* is false. If there is a relevant error that one is motivated to avoid in these cases, it might just be the error of acquiring a false belief about *p*, and sometimes circumstances are such that testing specifically for the truth of *p* is no easier or harder than testing specifically for its falsehood. In some such cases, one's thinking may accord with proper procedures and result in a belief about *p*. But, then, why should we suppose that one's thinking in these cases is motivated by a concern to minimize crucial errors as opposed to a concern to discover the truth (in an efficient way)? After all, one's cognitive conduct in these cases is consistent with each of the two competing motivational hypotheses. It may be suggested that given the evidence of PEDMIN motivation in other cases, there is a presumption in favor of its being present in these cases too. But, surely, it is possible that two different kinds of motivation are relevant to lay hypothesis testing—PEDMIN motivation and motivation to discover the truth about a proposition—and even that both kinds are simultaneously operative in some cases.

It might be claimed that motivation to discover the truth about *p* *is* PEDMIN motivation on the grounds that wanting to discover the truth about *p* is a matter of wanting to avoid certain errors—the error of not believing that *p* if *p* is true and the error of not believing that ~*p* if ~*p* is true. But this claim would undermine the contention that PEDMIN motivation, *as opposed to* motivation to discover the truth, is at work at a given time. The claim implies that when motivation to discover the truth is operative, it is an *instance* of PEDMIN motivation.

The cautionary points I have made are consistent with a moderate version of the FTL model's proving quite useful in understanding garden-variety self-deception. In section 1, I identified four ways in which our desiring that *p* can contribute to our believing that *p* in instances of self-deception: negative misinterpretation, positive misinterpretation, selective focusing or attending, and selective evidence-gathering. One aspect of the FTL model helps to explain why desires that *p* sometimes prompt and sustain cognitive activities of these kinds. People tend to test hypotheses in ways that minimize costly errors, and in the relevant range of cases, owing in part to the position occupied by a desire that *p* in the agent's motivational economy at the time, falsely believing that ~*p* would be a more costly error at the time than falsely believing that *p*. For example, when Don receives the rejection notice on his journal submission, he desires that the paper was wrongly rejected, and his motivational economy at the time is such that falsely believing that it was rightly rejected would be more costly "in terms of psychological discomfort" (Friedrich 1993, p. 314) than falsely believing that it was wrongly rejected. Thus, given that his evidence for the proposition that the paper was rightly rejected is not overwhelming, he will tend to interpret data in ways that increase the chance that he will believe that the paper was wrongly rejected.

This tendency helps us to understand how Don can acquire the belief that his paper was wrongly rejected in the face of considerable evidence to the contrary. Another aspect of the FTL model also contributes to such understanding. It is plausible that, as Trope and Liberman argue, we have "confidence thresholds" for the acceptance and rejection of propositions, that these thresholds are influenced by our desires in at least roughly the way they identify, and, accordingly, that we sometimes have an acceptance threshold for a proposition *p* that is significantly lower or higher than our rejection threshold for *p*. On the hypothesis that Trope and Liberman are right, it is likely that (at the relevant time) Don's threshold for believing that his paper was wrongly rejected is significantly lower than his threshold for believing that it was rightly rejected. Thus the probability that he will believe that it was wrongly rejected increases.

Although I have illustrated the two points just made with the example of Don's negative misinterpretation, the points also apply straightforwardly to positive misinterpretation and the two kinds of selectivity. Hypothesis testing encompasses not only the interpretation of data—including, sometimes, positive and negative misinterpretation—but also the gathering of data and attention to data. The tendency to test hypotheses in ways that minimize costly errors bears upon each of these aspects of hypothesis testing. And whether one of the two kinds of misinterpretation or selectivity or some combination thereof is at work, a lower acceptance threshold for *p* than for *~p* increases the probability that one will believe that *p*.

None of this entails that lay hypothesis testers sometimes try to deceive themselves, or try to make it easier for themselves to believe certain things. They test hypotheses in ways that are shaped by error costs, which in turn are shaped by their desires. Put a bit differently, they test hypotheses in ways that seem natural to them in the circumstances, and a major part of what makes their tests seem natural is relevant desire-shaped error costs. People's hypothesis testing behavior obviously has a significant effect on what they come to believe. Consequently, given the effects identified of desire on hypothesis testing, desire has an effect on belief acquisition. This effect neither requires nor entails an attempt on the part of hypothesis testers to deceive themselves into believing certain things or to make it easier for themselves to believe certain things.

Have I been overly bold in the preceding paragraph? Consider an agent who is averse to making a particular costly error, for example, the error of falsely believing that her son is guilty of treason. It may be claimed that if this aversion makes a causal contribution to her paying significantly more attention to evidence that supports the hypothesis that he is innocent than to contrary evidence and to her primarily seeking evidence of the former kind, the aversion must make this contribution in conjunction with a belief that behavior of these kinds will tend to help her avoid making the costly error at issue. And it may be claimed, accordingly, that the pertinent behavior is performed for a reason constituted by the aversion and instrumental belief just mentioned and that this behavior is therefore performed with the intention of avoiding, or of trying to avoid, making that error.

Are these claims correct? As I have indicated, Friedrich resists this interpretation of his version of the FTL model (1993, pp. 313, 317), but can it successfully be resisted? We can say that confidence thresholds are determined by the strength of aversions to specific costly errors together with information costs: setting aside "the cost of [gathering and processing] information," the stronger one's aversion to falsely believing that *~p*, the higher one's threshold for belief that *~p*. It is clear that, given a higher acceptance threshold for ~*p* than for *p*, belief that *p* is a more likely outcome than belief that ~*p*, other things being equal, because, other things being equal, lower thresholds are easier to reach than higher ones. This point certainly does not imply that aversions to costly errors motivate behavior performed with the intention of avoiding (or of trying to avoid) such errors. On the FTL model, however, such aversions also have effects on hypothesis testing that go beyond what is captured in the point about relative ease. They influence *how* we test hypotheses, not just *when we stop* testing them (owing to our having reached a relevant threshold). The example presently under investigation is a case in point, and recall the study in which subjects asked to adopt "the perspective of a cabin guard" showed an "extremely high frequency" of testing for disconfirming instances, whereas subjects asked to "take the perspective of a visitor" showed the common confirmation bias.

Are these further effects explicable only on the hypothesis that, owing partly to a belief about how to increase the probability that certain errors will be avoided, agents intentionally adopt certain strategies of error avoidance and test hypotheses as they do with the intention of avoiding, or of trying to avoid, those errors? As I have explained, desires have effects on the vividness and availability of data, which in turn have effects on belief acquisition, even though the believer does not try to produce any of these effects. As Friedrich suggests, desires to avoid specific errors may influence how we test hypotheses in the same general way. Such desires may trigger and sustain "automatic test strategies" (p. 313) in roughly the nonintentional way in which a desire that *p* results in the enhanced vividness of evidence for *p* or the increased availability of memorial evidence that *p*. A person's being more strongly averse to "false rejection" of the hypothesis that *p* than to "false acceptance" of it may have the effect that he primarily seeks evidence for *p*, is more attentive to such evidence than to evidence that ~*p*, and interprets relatively neutral data as supporting *p*, without this effect's being mediated by a belief that such behavior is conducive to avoiding the former error. The stronger aversion may simply frame the topic in such a way as to trigger and sustain these manifestations of the confirmation bias without the assistance of a belief that behavior of this kind is a means of avoiding certain errors. Similarly, having a stronger aversion that runs in the opposite direction may result in a skeptical approach to hypothesis testing that in no way depends on a belief to the effect that an approach of this kind will increase the probability of avoiding the costlier error. Given the aversion, skeptical testing is predictable quite independently of the agent's believing that a particular testing style will decrease the probability of making a certain error.

People may typically test hypotheses for "accuracy" in habitual, routinized ways. Which set of habits is activated or more strongly activated—habits associated with the confirmation bias or those associated with cheater detection, for example—may depend on which aversion of the pertinent kind is stronger. This pattern does not imply that agents, in these different scenarios, are executing intentions concerning different kinds of error avoidance (avoiding false rejection vs. avoiding false acceptance). Insofar as episodes of lay hypothesis testing are governed by a general intention, it may be an intention to locate, or to try to locate, the truth. That the way in which someone tests a particular hypothesis is influenced by aversions to error costs does not entail that he tests the hypothesis with the intention of reducing the probability that he will acquire a specific false belief.

Sometimes we do things that *are* means to certain ends without doing them *as* means to those ends. For example, while working on a philosophical paper, Ann, a normal mother with a normal mother's desire for her children's happiness, might find her thoughts drifting to her son's apparent unhappiness and its possible causes. Reflection about these things may be a means of putting herself in a position to help her son, but Ann may not be reflecting *as* a means of putting herself in a position to do this. Her thoughts may be drawn to the problem in the same involuntary way in which her thoughts are occasionally drawn to her mother's recent death. To reflect on a problem *as* a means of putting oneself in a position to resolve it is, in significant part, to think about it because one wants to resolve it and believes that reflection on it is a means to this end. Ann's current reflection on her son's problem may occur without the assistance of such a belief, just as some instances of her reflecting on her mother's death are not even partly explained by instrumental beliefs of hers. Similarly, behavioral manifestations of the confirmation bias may *be* means of avoiding certain errors without being performed *as* means of avoiding those errors. The same is true of some skeptical episodes of hypothesis testing.

It may be thought that, the FTL model notwithstanding, whenever such processes as positive or negative misinterpretation play an important role in the production of a motivationally biased belief that *p*, the agent is trying to bring it about that he believes that *p*, or at least is trying to make it easier for himself to believe that *p*. What else, one might ask, can explain the agent's misinterpreting the pertinent data as supporting *p* or as not (significantly) supporting *~p*?

Consider a natural application of the FTL model. If Sid, in an earlier example, has different confidence thresholds for acceptance and rejection of the hypothesis that Roz loves him, he might also have different confidence thresholds for acceptance and rejection of the following higher-order hypothesis: (*H*) Roz's refusing to date Sid and her reminding Sid that she loves Tim supports the hypothesis that she does not love Sid more strongly than it supports the hypothesis that she does love Sid. If Sid's rejection threshold for *H* is considerably lower than his acceptance threshold for it, he might come to reject *H*. He might view independent data that he regards as evidence that Roz loves him—for example, her regularly eating lunch with him and her friendliness toward him—as evidence that her refusals and reminders are not properly interpreted as supporting the hypothesis that she does not love him. An alternative construal of the refusals and reminders might suggest itself: Roz is playing hard to get in order to inspire Sid to prove that his love for her matches hers for him. Having a much lower threshold for accepting this new hypothesis than for rejecting it, and having some evidence for it while lacking conclusive evidence against it, Sid might come to believe that it is correct. There is no evident need to postulate exercises of agency of the sort urged by the "agency view" (ch. 1, sec. 3) to explain Sid's acquiring this belief.

It should also be observed that the project of explaining Sid's *retaining* this belief need not be significantly different from the project of explaining his acquiring it, even if the belief persists for quite some time. Processes of the same types that issue in the acquisition of motivationally biased, unwarranted beliefs may also subsequently play a role in sustaining those beliefs. For example, after he deceives himself into believing that Roz loves him, Sid may occasionally wonder whether his belief is true. Processes of the same kinds that issued in that belief may, on these occasions, be primed and shaped by relevant desires; and, of course, the salience and availability of data may be influenced by these desires even when Sid is not wondering whether Roz loves him. The general phenomenon of remaining in a state of self-deception does not require an explanation that is different in kind from a proper explanation of entering self-deception. More precisely, there is no need to suppose that the psychological mechanisms typically at work in the former phenomenon are different in kind from those typically at work in the latter. Often, of course, one's contrary evidence grows sufficiently strong that the belief that one is self-deceived in holding does not persist.

3. Attention and Inattention: A Problem for the FTL Model?

People sometimes are relatively inattentive to unpleasant evidence about themselves. Roy Baumeister and Kenneth Cairns (1992) found that, under certain conditions, some subjects spent less time reading such evidence than pleasant evidence about themselves. As Baumeister and Leonard Newman observe,

> the result obtained . . . only if the evaluation was confidential. Other subjects received identical feedback that was allegedly public, and they expected to have to interact with people who had access to that portrait of them. These subjects showed the opposite effect—that is, they spent *more* time reading their personality evaluations when these were unfavorable rather than favorable. Thought-listing data suggested that much of this extra time was used for thinking of ways to refute the disagreeable feedback. (1994, p. 12)

Are the results obtained by Baumeister and his colleagues inconsistent with the FTL model? And does the relative inattentiveness to unpleasant data under the confidentiality condition, or the marked difference between this and relative attentiveness under the nonconfidentiality condition, warrant the conclusion that subjects in the confidentiality condition tried to produce (or maintain) certain beliefs in themselves or tried to make it easier for themselves to come (or continue) to believe preferred propositions?

I start with the former question. In some cases, as predicted by the FTL model, people spend much time and effort critically examining evidence for the proposition that has the higher threshold. Call these "*C* cases." Are there cases in which, although the relevant costs (including information costs) and thresholds are equivalent to those in some *C* cases and the people involved are no less intellectually capable of critical thought, these people nevertheless respond to evidence for the proposition with the higher threshold primarily with inattentiveness rather than critical examination? This obviously is an empirical question, but surely it is conceivable that there are such cases—"*NC* cases." Supposing that *NC* cases exist, do they falsify the FTL model?

Not necessarily. For example, in an *NC* case, the initial lower threshold for belief that *p* might already have been reached, and, accordingly, depending on the apparent strength of the evidence for ~*p*, that evidence may simply be deemed unworthy of attention. However, I am not concerned to defend the FTL model in its full generality. Suppose that it needs to be significantly modified to account for some *NC* cases. Would it follow that in some cases of this type people are trying to bring it about that they acquire a certain belief, or trying to make it easier for themselves to acquire that belief?

Not at all. Baumeister and Cairns (1992) acknowledge that their experiment produced relative inattentiveness to threatening information only in "repressors." (Subjects were classified as repressors or nonrepressors on the basis of their performance on anxiety and "social desirability" questionnaires.) Perhaps the repressors were inattentive to this information because they found exposure to it very *unpleasant*. Having an aversion to unpleasant information that motivates inattentiveness to that information certainly is not conceptually sufficient for having a desire to produce, or promote, or sustain a belief, which desire motivates the inattentiveness as part of an attempt of the sort at issue. The aversion can effectively produce inattentiveness without the person's trying to produce or protect a belief, as I explained in Chapter 1, section 3.

Turn to the finding that when repressors expect the threatening information to be given to someone with whom they will interact, they are quite attentive to it. Does this difference between repressors' behavior in nonconfidentiality and confidentiality conditions show that in the confidentiality condition repressors try—unconsciously or consciously—to produce a belief in themselves, or to protect a belief they already possess, by means of inattentiveness? No. Their aversion to unpleasant information may be overridden by a desire to be well prepared to refute the psychological portrait of them presented to the other person. The aversion's being overridden when they expect the information to be made public is quite consistent with its operating in the confidentiality condition without the repressors' trying to produce or protect favored beliefs. Trying to avoid the unpleasant experience of attending to unpleasant feedback about oneself is one thing and trying to produce or protect a pleasant belief about oneself is another, even if attempts merely to avoid such experiences sometimes promote the acquisition or retention of such beliefs.

My guiding concern in the present chapter has been to explain how representative examples of garden-variety straight self-deception—the examples of Don and Sid, for instance—can be accounted for in terms of relatively well-understood psychological processes in a way that does not require an intention or attempt to deceive oneself, or to make it easier for oneself to believe something. The account offered fits what, in Chapter 1, I called the antiagency view, not the agency view. The explanation offered is supported further in the next two chapters, where I also argue that agency models of garden-variety straight self-deception have little to recommend them.

3

Self-Deception without Puzzles

ANALYZING SELF-DECEPTION is a difficult task; providing a plausible set of sufficient conditions for self-deception is less demanding. Not all cases of self-deception need involve the acquisition of a new belief. Sometimes we may be self-deceived in retaining a belief that we were not self-deceived in acquiring. Still, the primary focus in the literature has been on self-deceptive belief acquisition, and that is my focus in this book. In the present chapter, I motivate a statement of conceptually sufficient conditions for entering self-deception in acquiring a belief and I defend resolutions of the primary static and dynamic puzzles about self-deception (ch. 1, sec. 2). I also examine the phenomenon of entering self-deception in retaining a belief and tackle some "extreme" cases of straight self-deception.

1. SUFFICIENT CONDITIONS FOR ENTERING SELF-DECEPTION

I suggest that the following conditions are jointly sufficient for *entering self-deception in acquiring a belief that p*.

1. The belief that *p* which *S* acquires is false.
2. *S* treats data relevant, or at least seemingly relevant, to the truth value of *p* in a motivationally biased way.

3. This biased treatment is a nondeviant cause of *S*'s acquiring the belief that *p*.
4. The body of data possessed by *S* at the time provides greater warrant for ~*p* than for *p*.

Each condition requires brief attention. Condition 1 captures a purely lexical point. A person is, by definition, *deceived in* believing that *p* only if *p* is *false*; the same is true of being *self-deceived in* believing that *p*. The condition in no way implies that the falsity of *p* has special importance for the *dynamics* of self-deception. Motivationally biased treatment of data may sometimes result in someone's believing an improbable proposition, *p*, that, as it happens, is *true*. There may be self-deception in such a case, but the person is not self-deceived in believing that *p*, or in acquiring the belief that *p*.[1]

My discussion of various ways of entering self-deception serves well enough as an introduction to condition 2. My list of motivationally biased routes to self-deception is not intended as exhaustive, but my discussion of these routes does provide assistance in interpreting the notion of motivationally biased treatment of data.

My inclusion of the term "nondeviant" in condition 3 is motivated by a familiar problem for causal characterizations of phenomena in any sphere (see, e.g., Mele 1992, ch. 11). Specifying the precise nature of nondeviant causation of a belief by motivationally biased treatment of data is a difficult technical task better reserved for another occasion. However, much of this book provides guidance on the issue.

The thrust of condition 4 is that self-deceivers believe against the weight of the evidence they possess. I do not view condition 4 as a *necessary* condition of self-deception. In some instances of motivationally biased evidence-gathering, for example, people may bring it about that they believe a falsehood, *p*, when ~*p* is much better supported by evidence readily available to them, even though, owing to the selectivity of the evidence-gathering process, the evidence that they themselves actually *possess* at the time favors p over $\sim p$. Such people are naturally deemed self-deceived, other things being equal. However, some philosophers require that a condition like 4 be satisfied (e.g., Davidson 1985; McLaughlin 1988; Szabados 1985), and I have no objection to including condition 4 in a list of jointly *sufficient* conditions. Naturally, in some cases, whether the weight of a person's evidence lies on the side of p or of $\sim p$ (or equally supports each) is subject to legitimate disagreement.

Some philosophers have argued that my four conditions are insufficient because they do not capture a kind of *tension* that is necessary for self-deception. As Robert Audi understands this tension, "it is ordinarily represented . . . by an avowal of p . . . *coexisting* with knowledge or at least true belief that $\sim p$" (1997, p. 104). Michael Losonsky contends that self-deceivers have the unwarranted, false belief that p, lack the true belief that $\sim p$, and possess evidence for $\sim p$ that is "active" in their "cognitive architecture" (1997, p. 122). This activity, he claims, is manifested in such indications of tension as recurrent or nagging doubts, and he uses the contention that self-deception conceptually requires such conflict to support a distinction between self-deception and instances of "prejudice" or "bias" that satisfy the quartet of conditions I offered as conceptually sufficient for entering self-deception. Mike W. Martin mentions a similar tension, "a cognitive conflict" such as "suspecting p and believing $\sim p$" (1997, p. 123). And Kent Bach contends that self-deception requires actively avoiding or suppressing certain thoughts, or ridding oneself of these thoughts when they occur (1997; cf. Bach 1998, pp. 167–68).

The quartet of conditions I offered certainly does not entail that there is no tension in self-deception. Nor do I claim that self-deception normally is tension-free. Satisfying my four conditions may *often* involve considerable psychic tension. The present question is whether any of the alleged kinds of tension is conceptually *necessary* for entering self-deception in acquiring a belief that p. The answer is no. Given the details of Don's case, for example, even if he is free of psychic conflict during the process of acquiring the belief that his article was unjustly rejected and while that belief is in place, he is self-deceived and he enters self-deception in acquiring that belief. The same is true of bigots who, without psychic conflict, satisfy my four conditions in acquiring a bigoted belief that *p*.

Some theorists will insist that condition 4 is too weak and argue for a strengthened version that attributes to *S* a *recognition* that his evidence provides greater warrant for ~*p* than for *p*. It sometimes is claimed that, while we are deceiving ourselves into believing that *p*, we must be aware that our evidence favors ~*p*, on the grounds that this awareness is part of what explains our motivationally biased treatment of data (Davidson 1985, p. 146; Sackeim and Gur 1997, p. 125). The thought is that without this awareness we would have no reason to treat data in a biased way, because the data would not be viewed as threatening, and consequently we would not engage in motivationally biased cognition. Advocates of this thesis tend to understand self-deception on the model of *intentional action*: the agent has a goal, sees how to promote it, and seeks to promote it in that way.[2] However, the model places excessive demands on self-deceivers. Again, cold or unmotivated biased cognition is not explained on the model of intentional action, and motivation can prime and sustain the functioning of mechanisms for the cold biasing of data in us without our being aware, or believing, that our evidence favors a certain proposition. Desire-influenced biasing may result both in our not being aware that our evidence favors ~*p* over *p* and in our acquiring the belief that *p*. This is a natural interpretation of the illustrations I offered of misinterpretation and of selective focusing or attending (ch. 2, sec. 1). In each case, the person's evidence may favor the undesirable proposition; but there is no need to suppose the person is aware of this in order to explain the person's biased cognition.[3] Evidence that a scholarly paper one painstakingly produced is seriously flawed or that someone one loves lacks reciprocal feelings may be threatening even if one lacks the belief, or the awareness, that that evidence is stronger than one's contrary evidence.

Annette Barnes contends that a necessary condition of being self-deceived in believing that *p* is that "the purpose of one's believing that *p* is to reduce [some relevant] anxiety" (1997, p. 117).[4] Barnes explains that someone "has an anxious desire that *q* . . . just in case the person both desires that *q* and is anxious that it is not the case that *q*" (p. 38). She adds: "When a person is anxious that ~*q*, the person (1) is uncertain whether *q* or ~*q* and (2) desires that *q*. So a simpler analysis is also correct: one has an anxious desire that *q* just in case one is anxious that ~*q*" (p. 39).[5] Furthermore, in Barnes's attempted analysis of self-deception, an anxious desire that *q* is to be understood as a wholly intrinsic desire: "the person desires that *q* for its own sake and not for the sake of something else" (p. 39).

Barnes gives the distinct impression that anxiety that ~*q* is *identifiable* with a relevant uncertainty and a relevant desire: "To be anxious that ~*q* is to be uncertain whether *q* or ~*q* and to desire that *q* . . . for its own sake" (p. 67). But one wonders whether this is all there is to anxiety that ~*q*. If being anxious entails *feeling* anxious, the answer is no. I am a big fan of the Detroit Lions. I intrinsically desire that they have a fine record next season and I am uncertain whether they will, but I do not *feel* any anxiety about this. Although I may occasionally feel anxious about the Lions' record during the season, I have no such feelings now.

Barnes writes, "[Mele's] account differs in an important respect from both mine and [Mark] Johnston's. Whereas Mele assigns the pivotal causal role in self-deception to desire, I follow Johnston in assigning that role to *anxious* desire" (p. 37). "Mele . . . does not require, as I do, that the motivational work be done by anxiety" (p. 57). However, if an anxious desire is identifiable with an uncertainty and desire complex of the kind Barnes specifies, then, as I will explain, the statement of sufficient conditions for self-deception that I offered in this section suggests that the desires that play a role in producing the pertinent "motivationally biased" treatment of data are what Barnes calls "anxious desires," and Barnes's position on self-deception is even more similar to mine than she realizes.

Notice that *while* one believes that *p*, one cannot *acquire* the belief that *p*. And if one is certain that *p*, one believes that *p*. In conjunction with these obvious points, my conditions 1 and 3 each entail that, at least prior to deceiving himself, *S* is not certain that *p*. Now, to be sure, not being certain that *p* does not entail being *uncertain* that *p*. Bricks are neither certain nor uncertain about anything. Even so, my condition 2 suggests, at least, that beyond not being certain that *p*, prospective self-deceivers are uncertain that *p*. For it is psychologically very plausible that motivational biasing of the kind at issue there will occur only in a person who is uncertain that *p*. So, in my account, the focal desires in garden-variety straight self-deception seemingly are anxious ones, on the thin interpretation of "anxious desire" presently under consideration.

If Barnes is simply mistaken in thinking that the reference to an anxious desire in her account makes it importantly different from my account, that is just a matter of faulty bookkeeping. Partly because she is confident that her appeal to an anxious desire does add something important, however, I am inclined to believe that she takes the relevant anxiety to be more than just an uncertainty/desire complex. I am uncertain what she might want to add to the mix, but a very natural element to add is an *affective* component. One might hold that having an anxious desire that *q* entails *feeling* anxious that ~*q*. And perhaps "anxiety that ~*q*"—the state that it is "the purpose of one's believing that *p* . . . to reduce" in all cases of self-deception, on Barnes's view—is something essentially affective that essentially involves uncertainty and desire. But is anxiety, on a construal of this kind, involved in *all* cases of self-deception, and is "the purpose" of self-deceptive belief-formation *always* to reduce anxiety, in this sense?[6] Can it happen that someone who desires that *p* and is uncertain that *p* becomes self-deceived that *p* without ever *feeling* anxious that ~*p*? If there are conceptual grounds for a negative answer to this last question, Barnes does not say what they are. Nor does she offer empirical grounds for the empirical thesis that, in actual human beings, anxious feelings play an indispensable role in self-deception. Is it conceptually or psychologically impossible that I come to be self-deceived in believing that the Lions will have a good season before I have any anxious feelings about their season? I doubt it. Consequently, I have not made the presence of anxious feelings a necessary condition of self-deception.

Robert Audi has claimed that "self-deception is not a *historical* concept. If I am self-deceived, so is my perfect replica at the very moment of his creation" (1997, p. 104). Although this claim is not a threat to the assertion that my four conditions are conceptually *sufficient* for self-deception, it merits attention in this connection. Some concepts are historical in Audi's sense, and I take self-deception to be among them. The concept "sunburn" has a historical component. The burn on my back is a sunburn only if it was produced by exposure to the sun; a burn produced by a heat lamp that looks and feels just the same is not a sunburn. Some psychological concepts also are historical in this sense. Consider the concept "remembering" (as opposed to "seeming to remember"). My perfect replica at the moment of his creation does not remember being hired by my college; one cannot (actually) remember something that has never happened. Similarly, as I understand self-deception, beings who have not deceived themselves are not self-deceived, or in a state of self-deception, no matter what else is true of them.

2. Self-Deception in Retaining a Belief

The conditions for self-deception that I have offered are conditions specifically for entering self-deception in *acquiring* a belief. As I mentioned, however, ordinary conceptions of the phenomenon allow people to enter self-deception in *retaining* a belief. Here is an illustration. Sam has believed for many years that his wife, Sally, would never have an affair. In the past, his evidence for this proposition was quite good. Sally obviously adored him, she never displayed a sexual interest in another man, she condemned extramarital sexual activity, she was secure, she was happy with her family life, and so on. However, things recently began to change. Sally is now arriving home late from work on the average of two nights a week, she frequently finds excuses to leave the house alone after dinner and on weekends, and Sam has been informed by a close friend that Sally has been seen in the company of a certain Mr. Jones at a theater and a local lounge. Nevertheless, Sam continues to believe that Sally would never have an affair. But he is wrong. Her relationship with Jones is by no means platonic.

In general, the stronger the perceived evidence one has against a proposition that one believes (or "against the belief," for short), the harder it is to retain the belief. Suppose that Sam's evidence against his favored belief—that Sally is not having an affair—is not so strong as to render self-deception psychologically impossible and not so weak as to make an attribution of self-deception implausible. Plausibly, falsely believing that Sally is guilty of infidelity would be more costly (in the FTL sense) for Sam than falsely believing that she is innocent of this. So if the FTL model is on the right track, not only will Sam have a lower threshold for belief in Sally's innocence than for belief in her guilt, but he will also tend to conduct himself in ways that reduce the probability of his making the costlier error. Each of the four types of data manipulation that I have mentioned (ch. 2, sec. 1) may occur in a case of this kind. Sam may positively misinterpret data, reasoning that if Sally were having an affair she would want to hide it and that her public meetings with Jones consequently indicate that she is *not* sexually involved with him. He may negatively misinterpret data, and even (nonintentionally) recruit Sally in so doing by asking her for an "explanation" of the data or by suggesting for her approval some acceptable hypothesis about her conduct. Selective focusing may play an obvious role. And even selective evidence-gathering has a potential place in Sam's self-deception. He may set out to conduct an impartial investigation, but, owing to his desire that Sally not be having an affair, locate less accessible evidence for the desired state of affairs while overlooking some more readily attainable support for the contrary judgment.

Here again, garden-variety self-deception is explicable independently of the assumption that self-deceivers manipulate data in an attempt to deceive themselves, or in an effort to protect or produce a favored belief. Nor is there an explanatory need to suppose that at some point Sam both believes that *p* and believes that ~*p*.

Christian Perring has urged his readers to consider a modified version of this case, in which Sam decides not to think about the evidence of Sally's infidelity and intentionally occupies himself with other activities (1997).[7] "Sam does this to maintain his calmness and to avoid the pain of thinking about another divorce. . . . [T]he search for truth takes second place to his need to maintain psychological equilibrium" (p. 123). Perring contends that, in this version of the case, Sam intentionally deceives himself. He claims, as well, that Sam's "intentional self-deception is not self-defeating, but this is not because the intention to avoid thinking further about the evidence he has is hidden from him. It [the intention] is quite explicit."

As I explained in Chapter 1, an agent can intentionally do something, *A*, without intentionally bringing about some result that *A* has. Perring's modified example about Sam provides another illustration of this possibility. Sam's intentionally refraining from thinking about the evidence can have the result that he continues to believe (falsely) that Sally is not having an affair without his having intentionally brought it about that he continues to believe this and without his having intentionally deceived himself. The crucial question is this. What is Sam up to in intentionally refraining from thinking about this evidence? What is he trying to do in so conducting himself? (See ch. 1, sec. 3.) *Perhaps* he is trying to protect his belief in Sally's fidelity and trying to deceive himself into holding on to this belief. If he is, the dynamic paradox looms large and an appeal to an *unconscious* attempt is in the offing. However, there is no evident need to take this explanatory route. Our hypothetical data about Perring's version of Sam's case are entirely consistent with the hypothesis that, in intentionally refraining from thinking about the evidence at the time, Sam is merely trying, as Perring puts it, "to maintain his calmness and to avoid the pain of thinking about another divorce." Sam's aim may simply be to put off for a while the painful process of reflecting on evidence for a painful prospect. This hypothesis is utterly intelligible and theoretically unproblematic, and there is no shortage of empirical evidence for the claim that people are averse to pain, including painful reflection. A theorist who offers the alternative, "intentionality" hypothesis bears at least the burden of showing that it is no less plausible than the one just mentioned. I have more to say about this both in the present chapter and in the following one.

3. The Static and Dynamic Puzzles

I return to the familiar puzzles about self-deception described in Chapter 1, section 2. My resolutions of both puzzles highlighted there are implicit in what I have already said.

The main assumption that motivates the primary static puzzle, again, is this: by definition, person *A* deceives person *B* (where *B* may or may not be the same person as *A*) into believing that *p* only if *A* knows, or at least believes truly, that ~*p* and causes *B* to believe that *p*.[8] I have already argued that the assumption is false and have attacked two related conceptual claims about self-deception: that all self-deceivers know or believe truly that ~*p* while (or before) causing themselves to believe that *p*, and that they simultaneously believe that ~*p* and believe that *p*. In many garden-variety instances of self-deception, the false belief that *p* is not preceded by the true belief that ~*p*. Rather, a desire-influenced treatment of data has the result both that the person does not acquire the true belief and that he or she does acquire (or retain) the false belief. And, as I will argue further in Chapter 4, we lack good grounds for holding that there are cases of self-deception in which the two beliefs are possessed simultaneously.

I turn now to the dynamic puzzle. Here is a short version: if prospective self-deceivers have no strategy, how can they succeed? And if they do have a strategy, how can their attempt to carry it out fail to be self-undermining in garden-variety cases? Now, it may be granted that self-deception typically is *strategic* at least in the following sense: when people deceive themselves, they at least normally do so by engaging in potentially self-deceptive behavior, including cognitive behavior of the kinds catalogued in Chapter 2, section 1 (i.e., the two kinds of misinterpretation and the two kinds of selectivity). Behavior of these kinds can be counted, in a broad sense of the term, as *strategic*, and the behavioral types may be viewed as *strategies* of self-deception. Such strategies divide broadly into two kinds, depending on their locus of operation. *Internal-biasing* strategies feature the manipulation of data that one already has. Positive and negative misinterpretation are strategies of this kind. *Input-control* strategies feature one's controlling (to some degree) which data one acquires.[9] Selective evidence-gathering is a prime example. There are also *mixed* strategies, involving both internal biasing and input control. One may selectively focus, for example, both on certain data that one already has and on things in the external world. Do strategies of self-deception of these kinds depend for their effectiveness upon agents' employing them in an attempt to deceive themselves or in an effort to make it easier for themselves to believe a favored proposition? If so, how can the attempt fail to undermine itself? Will not the agents' knowledge of what they are up to get in the way? And, if prospective self-deceivers do not try to deceive themselves, or to make it easier for themselves to believe certain things, how can they possibly succeed? This is a fuller statement of the puzzle.

The resolution implicit in what I have been arguing admits of a simple formulation. First, in garden-variety cases of self-deception, strategies of the kinds at issue are not rendered ineffective by agents' intentionally exercising them with the knowledge of what they are up to; for, in garden-variety cases, self-deceivers do not intend or try to deceive themselves, or to make it easier for themselves to believe things. Second, because we can understand how causal processes that issue in garden-variety instances of self-deception function without the agent's intentionally orchestrating the process, we avoid the other horn of the puzzle as well. I turn now to further defense of this resolution.

Evidence that agents desirous of its being the case that *p* eventually come to believe that *p* owing to a biased treatment of data is sometimes regarded as supporting the claim that these agents intended to deceive themselves. The biasing apparently is sometimes relatively sophisticated purposeful behavior, and one may assume that such behavior must be guided by an intention of this kind. As I have argued, however, the sophisticated behavior in garden-variety examples of self-deception (e.g., Sam's case in sec. 2) may be accounted for on a less demanding hypothesis that does not require the agents to possess relevant intentions: for example, intentions to deceive themselves into believing that *p*, or to cause themselves to believe that *p*, or to make it easier for themselves to believe that *p*. Once again, motivational states can prompt and sustain biased cognition of the sorts common in self-deception without the assistance of such intentions. In Sam's case, a powerful motivational attraction to the hypothesis that Sally is not having an affair—in the absence both of a strong desire to ascertain the truth of the matter and of conclusive evidence of Sally's infidelity—may prompt and sustain the line of reasoning described earlier and the other belief-protecting behavior. An explicit, or consciously held, intention to deceive himself in these ways into holding on to his belief in Sally's fidelity would tend to undermine the project; and a hidden intention to deceive is not required to produce these activities. The same is true of the more modest intentions mentioned in this paragraph.

Even if this is granted, it may be held that the supposition that intentions of the kind at issue always or typically are at work in cases of self-deception is required to explain why a motivated biasing of data occurs in some situations but not in other very similar situations (Talbott 1995, pp. 60–62; cf. Talbott 1997; Bermudez 1997). Return to Don, who is self-deceived in believing that his article was wrongly rejected. At some point, while revising his article, Don may have wanted it to be true that the paper was ready for publication, that no further work was necessary. Given the backlog of work on his desk, he may have wanted that just as strongly as he later wanted it to be true that the paper was wrongly rejected. Further, Don's evidential situation at these two times may have been very similar: for example, his evidence that the paper was ready may have been no weaker than his later evidence that the paper was wrongly rejected, and his evidence that the paper was not ready may have been no stronger than his later evidence that the paper was rightly rejected. Still, we may suppose, although Don deceived himself into believing that the article was wrongly rejected, he did not deceive himself into believing that the article was ready for publication: he kept working on it—searching for new objections to rebut, clarifying his prose, and so on—for another week. To account for the difference in the two situations, it may be claimed, we must suppose that in one situation Don intended to make it easier for himself to believe the favored proposition (without being aware of this), whereas in the other he had no such intention. If the execution of self-deceptive biasing strategies were a non-intended consequence of being in a motivational and evidential condition of a certain kind, the argument continues, then Don would either have engaged in such strategies on both occasions or on neither: again, to account for the difference in his cognitive behavior on the earlier and later occasions, we need to suppose that an intention to bias his beliefs was at work in one case and not in the other.

This argument is flawed. If on one of the two occasions Don has a biasing intention whereas on the other he does not, then, presumably, some difference in the two situations accounts for *this* difference. But if there is a difference, *D*, in the two situations aside from the difference in intention that the argument alleges, an argument is needed for the claim that *D* itself cannot account for Don's self-deceptively biasing data in one situation and his not so doing in the other. Given that a difference in intention across situations (presence in one vs. absence in the other) requires some additional difference in the situations that would account for this difference, why should we suppose that there is no difference in the situations that can account for Don's biasing data in one and not in the other in a way that does not depend on his intending to bias data in one but not in the other? Why should we think that *intention* is involved in the explanation of the primary difference to be explained? Why cannot the primary difference be explained instead, for example, by Don's having a strong desire to avoid *mistakenly* believing the paper to be ready (or to avoid submitting a paper that is not yet ready) and his having at most a weak desire later to avoid mistakenly believing that the paper was wrongly rejected? Such a desire, in the former case, may block any tendency to bias data in a way supporting the hypothesis that the paper is ready for publication.

The FTL model of everyday hypothesis testing bears directly on the questions just raised. Return to the CIA agent—I call him Gordon—who was accused of treason (ch. 2, sec. 2). His staff of intelligence agents may very much want it to be true that he is innocent. After all, they are at much less personal risk if Gordon is innocent than if he has been betraying them, and some of them may be quite fond of him. Even so, many of them who have roughly the same evidence as Gordon's parents may not come to the conclusion that Gordon's parents reach—namely, that Gordon is innocent. They may instead conclude that he is guilty. Under the conditions described, why might his staff not reach the same conclusion as his parents? Did his parents intend or try to make it easier for themselves to believe that he is innocent, whereas his staff did not?

Here it is important to bear in mind a distinction between the cost of believing that *p* and the cost of believing *falsely* that *p*. The latter cost, not the former, is directly relevant to the determination of confidence thresholds in the FTL model. For Gordon's parents, the cost of believing falsely that their son is innocent may not differ much from the cost of believing that he is innocent (independently of the truth or falsity of this belief). We may suppose that believing that he is innocent has no cost for them. Indeed, the belief is a source of comfort, and believing that Gordon is guilty would be quite painful. Additionally, their believing *falsely* that he is innocent may pose no subjectively significant threat to the parents. With Gordon's staff, however, matters are very different. The cost to fellow agents of believing falsely that Gordon is innocent may be enormous, for they recognize that their lives are in his hands, even if they very much want it to be true that he is innocent.[10] Consequently, on the FTL view, we may expect the thresholds of Gordon's staff to diverge widely from his parents' thresholds. His parents have a much lower threshold for accepting the hypothesis that Gordon is innocent than for rejecting it, whereas in light of the relative costs of "false acceptance" and "false rejection" for his fellow agents, one would expect their thresholds to be quite the reverse of this. So here we have a significant, explanatorily relevant difference between the parents and the staff that is clearly an alternative to an alleged difference of the sort Talbott urges. On the FTL model, given the difference in thresholds, there is no need to suppose that Gordon's parents intended or tried to bias their cognitive processes in order to explain why they, unlike Gordon's staff, believed Gordon to be innocent of treason. (See ch. 2, sec. 2.)[11]

Presumably, at least some intentionalists will not be satisfied. They may claim (1) that there are pairs of cases in which the people involved have exactly similar confidence thresholds and evidence, but one person—the self-deceived one—ends up believing that *p* and the other does not. And they may claim (2) that, to account for the difference, we must suppose that the self-deceiver had a relevant intention—an intention to bring it about that he acquires a certain belief, or to make it easier for himself to acquire that belief, or the like—that the other person lacked. Now, if claim 1 is true, confidence thresholds, the desires and other psychological states that account for the thresholds, and evidence do not provide the whole explanatory story. Of course, I did not say that they did. Intelligence and intellectual training, for example, also are relevant. No one currently is able to provide an adequate *complete* account of the etiology of self-deception. The complexity of the phenomenon outstrips our knowledge. Before I return to this point, a related point requires emphasis.

Consider the claim that what accounts for the difference between the two members of the pair of cases at issue is that the self-deceiver intended to bring it about that he believed that *p* and the other person had no such intention. Now, many things that we intend to do, we do not do. Set aside intentions that we abandon before the time for action arises and intentions that we do not live long enough to execute. Often, we fail to perform intended actions that we try to perform. Just today, Helen intended to sink an easy shot on her favorite pool table, and she missed. A bit earlier, Al intended to take a twenty-one ounce cue stick from the wall rack but mistakenly pulled out a nineteen ounce stick instead. I see no reason to believe that people's intentions to bring it about that they acquire certain beliefs, or to make it easier for themselves to acquire certain beliefs, or to deceive themselves into believing that *p*—their "*B* intentions," for short—are more effective than their intentions to perform simple actions of the kinds mentioned. Indeed, I should think that their *B* intentions would be much less reliably executed, given the relative difficulty of the tasks. If that is right, then the intentionalist position faces its own "selectivity problem" (Bermudez 1997). If people have *B* intentions, there are cases in which they succeed in doing what they intend (e.g., Ike's case in ch. 1, sec. 3) and cases in which they do not. Why do people who have these intentions acquire the pertinent beliefs in some cases but not in others? Intentionalists have not answered this question, a slight variant of a question some of them raise for their opponents. Of course, an intentionalist might offer to answer the question with the assertion that *B* intentions are efficacious in the former cases but not in the latter. However, that obviously raises a question of the same kind: why are *B* intentions effective in some cases and not others?

Intentionalists can try to construct a more robust explanatory story that includes *B* intentions and other elements, including elements that allegedly explain why the effective intentions are successfully executed whereas the others are not. Ironically, identification of the additional elements may support the idea that there is no need to insist on the presence of *B* intentions in typical self-deception. The additional elements combined with relevant desires, confidence thresholds, evidence, our background knowledge about various biases, and the like may turn the trick without the assistance of *B* intentions.

At this point, proponents of the thesis that self-deception is intentional deception or requires an attempt to increase the probability that one believes a favored proposition apparently need to rely on claims about the explanatory place of intentions or biasing efforts in self-deception itself, as opposed to their place in explaining differences across situations. Claims of that sort have already been evaluated here, and they have been found wanting.

Consciously executing an intention to deceive oneself is possible, as in the case of Ike (the man, described in ch. 1, sec. 3, who doctored his own diary); but such cases are remote from paradigmatic examples of self-deception. Executing a "hidden" intention to deceive oneself, or to make it easier for oneself to believe something, may be possible, too; but, as I have argued, there is no good reason to maintain that such intentions are at work in paradigmatic self-deception. Part of what I have argued, in effect, is that some theorists have made self-deception more theoretically perplexing than it actually is by imposing on the phenomena a problematic conception of self-deception. The argument will be strengthened in Chapter 4.

4. Extreme Cases

We do not believe every proposition that we would like to be true. I would like it to be true that I currently am able to run a mile in less than four minutes and to complete a marathon in less than three hours. Even so, I do not believe that I am able to do these things; indeed, I know that I am not. The FTL model is entirely consistent with this general point. Even if my confidence threshold for a preferred proposition, *p*, is much lower than my threshold for ~*p*, it may not be so low that the evidence for *p* can get me to that threshold. However, it seems that there are straight cases of self-deception in which the gap between the weaker evidence for the preferred proposition, *p*, and the stronger evidence for ~*p* is quite large. Some readers may be inclined to suppose that even if much ordinary self-deception does not involve an attempt to deceive oneself or an effort to make it easier for oneself to believe a desired proposition, cases of the kind just mentioned *must* involve some such effort. They may think that a view of the kind I have been advancing is bound to fail in these extreme cases. Again, there is the danger that such exercises of agency would undermine themselves. And there is the predictable reply that that danger is avoided by the supposition that these are exercises that the agents are not conscious of making. Is an "agency" explanation featuring unconscious trying or an explanation of the sort offered by the FTL model more plausible in cases of the kind at issue?

Brief consideration of some extreme cases of self-deception should prove instructive. Consider the following case from a short story by Isaac Bashevis Singer, "Gimpel the Fool" (Singer 1953).

One night, Gimpel, a gullible man, enters his house after work and sees "a man's form" next to his wife in bed. He immediately leaves—in order to avoid creating an uproar that would wake his child, or so he says. The next day, his wife, Elka, denies everything, implying that Gimpel must have been dreaming. Their rabbi orders Gimpel to move out of the house, and Gimpel obeys. Eventually, Gimpel begins to long for his wife and child. His longing apparently motivates the following bit of reasoning: "Since she denies it is so, maybe I was only seeing things? Hallucinations do happen. You see a figure or a mannequin or something, but when you come up closer it's nothing, there's not a thing there. And if that's so, I'm doing her an injustice." Gimpel bursts out in tears. The next morning he tells his rabbi that he was wrong about Elka.

After nearly a year's deliberation, a council of rabbis inform Gimpel that he may return to his home. He is ecstatic, but wanting not to awaken his family, he walks in quietly after his evening's work. Predictably, he sees someone in bed with Elka, a certain young apprentice, and he accidentally awakens Elka. Pretending that nothing is amiss, Elka asks Gimpel why he has been allowed to visit and then sends him out to check on the goat, giving her lover a chance to escape. When Gimpel returns from the yard, he inquires about the absent lad. "What lad?" Elka asks. Gimpel explains, and Elka again insists that he must have been hallucinating. Elka's brother then knocks Gimpel unconscious with a violent blow to the head. When Gimpel awakes in the morning, he confronts the apprentice, who stares at him in apparent amazement and advises him to seek a cure for his hallucinations.

Gimpel comes to believe that he has again been mistaken. He moves in with Elka and lives happily with her for twenty years, during which time she gives birth to many children. On her deathbed, Elka confesses that she has deceived Gimpel and that the children are not his. Gimpel the narrator reports: "If I had been clouted on the head with a piece of wood it couldn't have bewildered me more." "Whose are they?" Gimpel asks, utterly confused. "I don't know," Elka replies. "There were a lot . . . but they're not yours." Gimpel sees the light.

On more than one occasion, Gimpel comes to believe that Elka has remained faithful to him. And even though Elka and others tried to deceive him into believing this, the reader cannot help but see Gimpel's belief in her fidelity as motivated (at least partly) by his feelings for her and by his desire that she has, in fact, been faithful. Moreover, Gimpel holds this belief even in the face of very strong evidence to the contrary. So this seems to be an extreme case of self-deception of the sort that my present question calls for. In order to explain Gimpel's acquiring his belief in Elka's fidelity, must we suppose that he tried to bring it about that he believed this, or that he tried to make it easier for himself to believe this?

No. As Gimpel's separation from Elka lengthens, his longing for her increases and the evidence of her infidelity becomes less vivid. The cost of believing falsely that Elka has been unfaithful becomes increasingly, and painfully, clear. Thus, on the FTL view, one would expect a significant decrease in Gimpel's confidence threshold for the hypothesis that she has been faithful. Given the lower threshold and dimmer evidence of infidelity, Gimpel's acquiring a belief in Elka's fidelity seems to be a genuine possibility, and there is no evident need to suppose that he acquired this belief by means of unconscious exercises of agency. Perhaps brighter people in Gimpel's shoes would not have come to his conclusion about Elka, but it is difficult to see why it should be thought that an "agency explanation" of Gimpel's belief is more plausible than the explanation generated by the FTL model.

It should also be observed that even though there are times when Gimpel believes that Elka has slept with another man and times when he believes that she has never done this, Singer does not imply that Gimpel ever simultaneously held both beliefs. Nor need we make this assumption to support the commonsense judgment that Gimpel was self-deceived. We can understand how, owing to selective focusing and the like, a person can lose the belief that *p* and then acquire the belief that *~p*. This seems to be what happens in Gimpel's case. First, he believes that Elka is unfaithful. Then, influenced by motivated attention to skeptical hypotheses, he abandons that belief, apparently withholding belief on the matter. Later, owing partly to further motivated treatment of data, he acquires the belief that she has always been faithful—a belief that he loses only when he comprehends the meaning of Elka's confession.

Amelie Rorty (1988, p. 11) has offered a putative example of self-deception that may seem to speak strongly in favor of the presence of unconscious true beliefs in some cases of self-deception. It may not be as extreme as Singer's example—after all, Gimpel twice caught his wife in bed with another man and yet came to disbelieve his eyes—but it features a character who is considerably brighter than simple Gimpel. Dr. Androvna, a cancer specialist, "has begun to misdescribe and ignore symptoms [of hers] that the most junior premedical student would recognize as the unmistakable symptoms of the late stages of a currently incurable form of cancer." She had been neither a particularly private person nor a financial planner, but now she "deflects [her friends'] attempts to discuss her condition [and] though young and by no means affluent, she is drawing up a detailed will." What is more, "never a serious correspondent, reticent about matters of affection, she has taken to writing effusive letters to distant friends and relatives, intimating farewells, and urging them to visit her soon."

If I had read Rorty's vignette out of context, I would have been confident that Androvna knew—quite consciously—that she had cancer but did not want to reveal that to others. That hypothesis certainly makes good sense of the details offered. (Singer's story, on the other hand, makes it plausible that Gimpel was self-deceived: plausibly, for many years, he believed that Elka had always been faithful—without also believing the opposite. Of course, Singer had the luxury of ample space to spin a good yarn.) Even so, it is conceivable that Androvna is self-deceived. If she is, what explains the detailed will and the effusive letters? Some will suggest that, "deep down," Androvna knows that she is dying and that this knowledge accounts for these activities. On the assumption that it is conceivable that Androvna does not consciously believe that she has cancer in the circumstances that Rorty describes, is it also conceivable that she does not unconsciously believe this either?

Yes, it is. Androvna's not believing, unconsciously or otherwise, that she has the disease is consistent with her consciously believing that there is a significant *chance* that she has it, and that belief, in conjunction with relevant desires, can lead her to make out a will, write the letters, and deflect questions. (Notice that she may be self-deceived in believing that there is *only* a significant chance that she has cancer.) Some theorists will ask, perhaps with a hint of satisfaction in their tone, whether, given Rorty's description of the case and the assumption that Androvna lacks the conscious belief that she has cancer, it is more likely (1) that she believes "deep down" that she has the disease (has a "type 1" cancer belief) or (2) that she consciously believes that there is a significant chance that she has cancer without also believing, deep down or otherwise, that she has it (has a "type 2" cancer belief). Base-rate information is relevant here. My students know that there are a great many more blue-collar workers than lawyers. Yet, when I ask them whether a man wearing a nice suit and a tie is more likely to be a lawyer or a blue-collar worker, most of them answer, "a lawyer"—at least until the relevance of base rates is made salient. What are the relative frequencies of type 1 and type 2 beliefs (i.e., "deep down," unconscious beliefs and beliefs that there is a significant chance that *p* that fall sort of being beliefs that *p*)?[12] Until one has at least a partial basis for an answer to this question that would help underwrite the judgment that Androvna believes deep down that she has cancer, one is not entitled to be confident that she has such a belief. Notice that it is quite evident that we have and act on a great many type 2 beliefs. For many of us, such beliefs help to explain why we purchase home insurance, for example, or take an umbrella to work when we read in the morning paper that there is a 30 percent chance of rain. Is there anything approaching comparably weighty evidence of frequent type 1 beliefs? If so, I am not aware of it. (Chapter 4 bears on this question.)

One may ask why, if Androvna believes that there is a significant chance that she is stricken with cancer, she does not seek medical attention. Recall that she knows the type of cancer at issue to be incurable; she may see little point in consulting fellow cancer specialists. Regardless of that detail, however, we know that procrastination about seeking medical attention is, unfortunately, an all too familiar phenomenon, and it does not require type 1 beliefs. People often wait too long to act on their type 2 beliefs in this sphere. Finally, as in Gimpel's case, there is no evident need to suppose that Androvna was *trying* to deceive herself. Her failing to believe that she has cancer is surprising, but no more surprising that Gimpel's failing to believe his eyes.

5. Conclusion

Advocates of the view that self-deception is essentially (or normally) intentional may seek support in a distinction between self-deception and *wishful thinking*. They may claim that although wishful thinking does not require an intention to deceive oneself, self-deception differs from it precisely in being intentional. This may be interpreted either as stipulative linguistic legislation or as a substantive claim. On the former reading, a theorist is simply expressing a decision to reserve the term "self-deception" for an actual or hypothetical phenomenon that requires an intention to deceive oneself or an intention to produce in oneself a certain belief. Such a theorist may proceed to inquire about the possibility of the phenomenon and about how occurrences of self-deception, in the stipulated sense, may be explained. On the latter reading, a theorist is advancing a substantive conceptual thesis—the thesis that *the* concepts (or our ordinary concepts) of wishful thinking and of self-deception differ along the lines mentioned.

I have already criticized the conceptual thesis about self-deception. A comment on wishful thinking is in order. If wishful thinking is not wishful *believing*, one difference between wishfully thinking that *p* and being self-deceived in believing that *p* is obvious. If, however, wishful thinking is wishful believing—in particular, motivationally biased, false believing—then, if it does not overlap with self-deception (an assumption challenged in Mele 1987a, p. 135), the difference may lie in the relative strength of relevant evidence against the believed proposition: wishful thinkers may encounter weaker counterevidence than self-deceivers (Szabados 1985, pp. 148–49). This difference requires a difference in *intention* only if the relative strength of the evidence against the propositions that self-deceivers believe is such as to require that their acquiring or retaining those beliefs depends on the operation of a pertinent intention. This thesis about relative evidential strength, as I have argued, is false.

Conceptual work on self-deception guided by the thought that the phenomenon must be largely isomorphic with stereotypical interpersonal deception has generated some much-discussed conceptual puzzles. But, I have argued, it also has led us away from a proper understanding of garden-variety straight self-deception. Stereotypical interpersonal deception is intentional deception; ordinary self-deception, I have argued, probably is not. If it were intentional, "hidden" intentions and attempts would be at work; and we lack good grounds for holding that such intentions or attempts are operative in garden-variety self-deception. Furthermore, in stereotypical interpersonal deception, there is some time at which the deceiver believes that ~*p* and the deceived believes that *p*; but there is no good reason to hold, I have argued, that self-deceivers simultaneously believe that ~*p* and believe that *p*. In light of these points, one should seek an explanatory model for self-deception that diverges from models for the explanation of intentional conduct. I am offering such a model.

Even in a case of self-deception as extreme as Gimpel's, there is no need to suppose that the agent tried to deceive himself, or to cause himself to believe the desired proposition, or to make it easier for himself to believe that proposition. Undoubtedly, some readers are toying with other extreme cases with which to test my position. Obviously, it is impossible to examine an endless series of cases of self-deception that are allegedly isomorphic in the relevant respects with stereotypical interpersonal deception. In the following chapter, however, I argue against the leading attempted empirical demonstrations of such self-deception.

4

Attempted Empirical Demonstrations of Strict Self-Deception

SOME PSYCHOLOGISTS have offered alleged empirical demonstrations of self-deception, on a strict conception of the phenomenon requiring that self-deceivers (at some point) simultaneously believe that *p* and believe that *~p*.[1] Seeing that and why influential work in this area has failed to hit its mark reinforces the position on garden-variety straight self-deception defended in the preceding two chapters. I name the alleged requirement at issue on self-deception the "dual-belief requirement." The condition at issue—that is, simultaneously believing that *p* and believing that *~p*—is the "dual-belief condition."

1. BACKGROUND

In a recent article (Mele 1997a), I challenge critics to provide convincing evidence of the existence of instances of self-deception that satisfy the dual-belief requirement. Explicitly leaving it open that the simultaneous possession of a pair of beliefs whose propositional contents are mutually contradictory is conceptually and psychologically possible (pp. 98–99), I argue that influential empirical work on the topic does not meet the challenge and that there is no explanatory need to postulate "dual beliefs" either in familiar cases of self-deception or in the empirical studies discussed. Because some of the researchers who took up my challenge were not careful to keep the dual-belief condition in focus, I begin by eliminating some unpromising lines of response before reviewing the more pertinent studies.

The thrust of some of the responses to my challenge is that certain empirical or theoretical results provide direct or indirect support for the idea that mental operations are layered, partitioned, or segmented in a way that favors the possibility or probability of someone's believing that *p* while also believing that ~*p*. I myself would like to see convincing evidence that this dual-belief condition is satisfied in some cases of self-deception. Such evidence would settle one significant question about self-deception, and it might even provide indirect support for my own belief that if there is self-deception of the dual-belief variety, it is remote from garden-variety instances. As I argue, however, the alleged evidence I have seen is unconvincing.

Some preliminary conceptual observations are in order. First, the large collection of propositions believed by a person at a time may well include inconsistencies. For example, the propositions someone believes now might include a collection of the following sort: if *q* then (*r* or *s*); *q*, *t*, and *u*; if (*t* or *u*) then ~*r*; if *u* then ~*s*. My concern is with believing that *p* (e.g., that Bob stole Ann's car) while also believing that ~*p* (that Bob did not steal Ann's car), for many have alleged that precisely this condition is necessary for self-deception.[2] Second, possessing a body of evidence that provides greater *warrant* for ~*p* than for *p* should not be confused with believing that ~*p*. We do not always believe the propositions that our evidence warrants. Third, some people use the term "belief" to refer both to *what* is believed (e.g., that Bob stole Ann's car) and to the associated *state of mind* (e.g., Ann's belief that Bob stole her car). As long as the two senses are not confused with one another, discussion can proceed smoothly. The propositions *p* and ~*p* are logically contradictory; that is, it is logically impossible that both *p* and ~*p* are true. This does not entail that it is logically impossible to believe that *p* while also believing that ~*p*.

Stephanie Brown and Douglas Kenrick offer alleged examples of logically contradictory propositions simultaneously believed by a person (1997, p. 109). The following is one: *S* may "believe alcohol has all the toxicity of strychnine" while also believing "that a few drops of the spirits can have all the benefits of ambrosia" (translation: a little alcohol can make one feel good). In fact, the two propositions are not logically contradictory: that alcohol has the toxicity of strychnine is consistent with its being true that a little alcohol can make one feel good. Nor is there any logical contradiction in the propositions involved in similar examples of theirs: for instance, the combination of "*S* is not having an affair" with propositions constituting evidence (but not entailing) that *S* is having an affair.

Brown and Kenrick offer another kind of example that is unpersuasive for another reason. They write, "we may be led to believe that 'free love' is a splendid idea while sexually aroused . . . and to believe precisely the opposite after viewing a film about AIDS" (p. 109). Now, surely, they do not want to claim that we never abandon any of our beliefs (there are many things I once believed that I no longer do). So why should we suppose that when the imagined people come to believe that free love is not a splendid thing, they still believe that it is a splendid thing? Furthermore, if they do simultaneously possess a relevant pair of beliefs about free love, one positive and the other negative, why should we maintain that the propositional contents are logically contradictory? Perhaps they believe that insofar as free love is pleasant, there is something to be said for it, while also believing that since free love is very dangerous, there is much to be said against it. These two propositions are mutually consistent.

Tim Dalgleish argues that "unexceptional cases of emotional self-deception . . . can involve holding two contradictory beliefs (*p* and ~*p*) at the same time" (1997, p. 110). He contends that "an individual can hold a propositional belief *p* while simultaneously having a higher-order emotional understanding of the situation consistent with ~*p*." However, to claim that *S* has a higher-order understanding that is consistent with ~*p*, or with *S*'s believing that ~*p*, is not yet to claim that *S* believes that ~*p*. Presumably, many propositions *consistent* with—that is, not contradicted by—our emotional understandings of things are not believed by us. (That there is intelligent life on Mars does not contradict Al's emotional understanding of his mother's recent death, because that understanding has no bearing on Mars; but Al does not believe that there is intelligent life on Mars.) So Dalgleish must, and does, go further.

He contends that someone might believe that his brother is honest while also "having a sense that in fact he is deceitful." But does this "sense" amount to or encompass a *belief* that his brother is deceitful, or is it merely a suspicion that he is deceitful or a belief that there is evidence that he is deceitful? Dalgleish also claims that "everyday conversation" indicates that "paradoxical conflict" of the sort at issue is common: people often say such things as "I know and believe that I'm a success at work because I only have to look at the evidence but deep down I still believe that I'm a failure" (p. 111). However, one must be careful in interpreting such assertions. Claims of this kind may well be metaphorical. Moreover, everyday conversation is influenced by everyday theories, many of which may be seriously misguided.

A familiar defense of the claim that self-deceived people satisfy the dual-belief condition proceeds from the premise that they behave in conflicting ways. For example, it is alleged that although self-deceivers like Sam (in ch. 3, sec. 2) sincerely assure their friends that their spouses are faithful, they normally treat their spouses in ways that manifest distrust. This is an empirical matter on which I cannot pronounce. But suppose, for the sake of argument, that the empirical claim is true. Even then, we would lack sufficient grounds for holding that, in addition to believing that their spouses are not having affairs, these self-deceivers also believe, simultaneously, that their spouses are so engaged. After all, the supposed empirical fact can be accounted for on the alternative hypothesis that, while believing that their spouses are faithful, these self-deceivers also believe that there is a significant chance they are wrong about this. The mere suspicion that one's spouse is having an affair does not amount to a *belief* that he or she is so involved. And one may entertain suspicions that *p* while believing that ~*p*.

An anonymous referee of my article (Mele 1997a) suggested that the phenomenon of "blindsight" involves the presence of a pair of beliefs whose propositional contents are mutually contradictory. There is evidence that some people who believe themselves to be blind can see (Weiskrantz 1986). They perform much better (and, in some cases, much worse) on certain tasks than they would if they were simply guessing, and steps are taken to ensure that they are not benefiting from any other sense. Suppose some sighted people in fact believe themselves to be blind. Do they also believe that they are sighted (not blind)? If it were true that all sighted people (even those who believe themselves to be blind) believe themselves to be sighted, the answer would be yes. But precisely the evidence for "blindsight" is evidence against the truth of this universal proposition. The evidence indicates that, under certain conditions, people have the power of sight without believing that they do and see something without believing that they are seeing.

The same referee appealed to a more mundane case of the following sort. Ann set her watch a few minutes ahead to promote punctuality. Weeks later, when we ask her for the time, Ann looks at her watch and reports what she sees, "11:10." We then ask whether her watch is accurate. If she recalls having set it ahead, she might sincerely reply, "No, it's fast; it's actually a little earlier than 11:10." Now, at time *t*, when Ann says "11:10," does she both believe that it is 11:10 and believe that it is not 11:10? There are various alternative possibilities. Perhaps, for example, although she has not forgotten setting her watch ahead, her memory of so doing is not salient for her at *t* and she does not infer at *t* that it is not 11:10; or perhaps she has adopted the strategy of *acting as if* her watch is accurate and does not actually *believe* any of its readings. (Defending a promising answer to the following question is left as an exercise for the reader: what would constitute convincing evidence that, at *t*, Ann believes that it is 11:10 and believes that it is not 11:10?)[3]

2. Voice Recognition and Hypnosis

Ruben Gur and Harold Sackeim propose the following statement of "necessary and sufficient" conditions for self-deception:

> 1. The individual holds two contradictory beliefs (*p* and ~*p*).[4]
> 2. These two contradictory beliefs are held simultaneously.
> 3. The individual is not aware of holding one of the beliefs (*p* or ~*p*).
> 4. The act that determines which belief is and which belief is not subject to awareness is a motivated act. (Sackeim and Gur 1978, p. 150; cf. Gur and Sackeim 1979; Sackeim and Gur 1985)

Because Sackeim and Gur adopt a conception of intentional action according to which an action is intentionally performed only if it "is planned, considered, or expected by" the agent, and because they, unlike David Pears, for example (see ch. 1, sec. 3), do not wish to postulate subagents, they "do not claim that the 'motivated act' [at issue in condition 4] is intentional" (1978, p. 150). Even so, they do say that the pertinent acts are "acts of deciding between which beliefs to endorse or which beliefs not to notice" (p. 149).[5] Thus, they are offering a relatively standard "agency" conception of self-deception (cf. Sackeim and Gur 1997). Naturally, Sackeim and Gur hold that the decisional acts at issue "are not themselves reflected upon" by the agent (1978, p. 149).

Sackeim and Gur's evidence for the occurrence of self-deception, as they define the phenomenon, is provided by voice-recognition studies. In one type of experiment, subjects who wrongly state that a tape-recorded voice is not their own, nevertheless show physiological responses (e.g., galvanic skin responses) that are correlated with voice recognition. "The self-report of the subject is used to determine that one particular belief is held," while "behavioral indices, measured while the self-report is made, are used to indicate whether a contradictory belief is also held" (Sackeim and Gur 1978, p. 173). (The experimenters also attempt to make a case for the satisfaction of the motivational condition.)

It is unclear, however, that the physiological responses are demonstrative of *belief* (Mele 1987b, p. 6).[6] In addition to believing that the voice is not their own (if we assume the reports are sincere), do the subjects also *believe* that it is their own, or do they merely exhibit physiological responses that often accompany the belief that one is hearing one's own voice? Perhaps there is only a *subdoxastic* (from *doxa* 'belief') sensitivity in these cases. The threshold for physiological reaction to one's own voice may be lower than that for cognition (including unconscious belief) that the voice is one's own. Furthermore, another team of psychologists (Douglas and Gibbins 1983; cf. Gibbins and Douglas 1985) obtained similar results for subjects' reactions to voices of *acquaintances*. Thus, even if the physiological responses were indicative of belief, they would not establish that subjects hold "contradictory" beliefs. Perhaps subjects believe that the voice is not their own while also "believing" that it is a familiar voice.

Irving Kirsch contends that many hypnotized people acquire "contradictory beliefs" (1997, p. 118).[7] He offers the following evidence. Many people "who displayed an apparent inability to bend an arm . . . indicated [1a] that they had tried to bend the arm and also [1b] that they could have bent their arm if they had really wanted to." Similarly, many "people who displayed suggested amnesia . . . claimed [2a] they wrote down every suggestion they could remember and [2b] that they could have remembered the suggestions if they really wanted to." If these people believed what they asserted, we must ask whether the propositions believed are contradictory.

There is no logical contradiction in the conjunction of 1a and 1b. Consider an analogy. After losing a close tennis match, one might believe (3a) that one tried to win and (3b) that one would have (and hence could have) won if one had really wanted to win. There is no contradiction in this pair of propositions: indeed, one might *reasonably* believe that one would have won if one had tried considerably harder to win and that if one had had a considerably stronger desire ("really wanted") to win one would have tried a lot harder. Notice that 3a and 3b have the same form as 1a and 1b: because the former pair is not contradictory, neither is the latter pair. And although bending an arm normally is quite easy, the tennis analogy may not be farfetched in the present context. For these hypnotized individuals, arm bending might have seemed to require a lot of effort, and more effort than they wanted to exert.

The comparable data about amnesia can be handled along the same lines, although the quoted claims are less precise. I take the subjects to mean that they wrote down every suggestion they consciously remembered, that they tried to remember, and that they could have remembered more suggestions if they had been more strongly desirous of doing so. This is a consistent set of propositions.

3. Quattrone and Tversky's Cold-Water Study: Background

George Quattrone and Amos Tversky, in an elegant study (1984), argue for the reality of self-deception satisfying Sackeim and Gur's four conditions. In this study, thirty-eight undergraduate subjects first submerged a "forearm into a chest of circulating cold water until they could no longer tolerate it" (1984, p. 240). "After every [five seconds] they reported a number from 1 to 10 to express their discomfort"; a rating of 10 designated "that point at which subjects would rather not tolerate the cold any longer" (p. 241). They then pedaled an exercycle for one minute. Next, during a brief "rest period," subjects were given a "mini-lecture on psychophysics" in which they were led to believe that people have either of two different "cardiovascular complexes, referred to as Type 1 and Type 2 hearts" and that shorter and longer life expectancies are associated, respectively, with "increasing degrees" of Type 1 and Type 2 hearts (p. 241). Subjects were then assigned randomly to either of two groups. Half "were informed that a Type 1 [unhealthy] heart would increase tolerance to cold water after exercise, whereas a Type 2 [healthy] heart would decrease tolerance" (p. 240). The rest were told the opposite. Finally, participants were subjected again to the "cold-pressor" trial, after which they completed a brief questionnaire. They were asked, among other things, the following question (p. 241): "Did you purposely try to alter the amount of time you kept your hand in the water after exercise?"[8]

As predicted, subjects who were told that decreased tolerance was diagnostic of a healthy heart "showed significantly less tolerance" on the second trial, "whereas subjects in the increase condition showed significantly more tolerance" on that trial (p. 242). Twenty-seven of the thirty-eight subjects showed the predicted shift. Only nine subjects indicated that they had tried to shift their tolerance. And only two of the nine (22 percent) who admitted this inferred that they had a Type 2 (healthy) heart, whereas twenty of the twenty-nine "deniers" (69 percent) inferred that they had a Type 2 heart.

Quattrone and Tversky contend that the majority of subjects *tried* to shift their tolerance on the second trial. Most subjects denied having tried to do this, and Quattrone and Tversky argue that many of their subjects believed that they did not try to shift their tolerance while also believing that they did try to shift it. They argue, as well, that these subjects were unaware of holding the latter belief, the "lack of awareness" being explained by their "desire to accept the diagnosis implied by their behavior" (p. 239).

4. Do Quattrone and Tversky's Subjects Satisfy the Dual-Belief Requirement?

In the present section, I assume for the sake of argument that many of Quattrone and Tversky's subjects did, in fact, try to shift their tolerance on the second trial and I argue that, even if this is so, we lack good reason to hold that they satisfied the alleged dual-belief requirement on self-deception. I argue in section 5 that there is no explanatory need to suppose that any of the sincere deniers were, in fact, trying to shift their tolerance.

Assume that many of the subjects tried to shift their tolerance in the second trial, that their attempts were motivated, and that most of the "deniers" *sincerely* denied having tried to shift their tolerance. Even on the supposition that the deniers were aware of their motivation to shift their tolerance, does it follow that, in addition to believing that they did not "purposefully engage in the behavior to make a favorable diagnosis," these subjects also believed that they did do this, as Quattrone and Tversky claim? Does anything block the supposition that the deniers were effectively motivated to shift their tolerance without believing, at any level, that this is what they were doing? (My use of "without believing, at any level, that [*p*]" is elliptical for "without believing that *p* while being aware of holding the belief and without believing that *p* while not being aware of holding the belief.")

The study does not offer any direct evidence that the sincere deniers believed that they were trying to shift their tolerance. Nor is the assumption that they believed this required to explain their behavior. (The required belief for the purpose of behavior explanation is a belief to the effect that a suitable change in one's tolerance on the second trial would constitute evidence of a healthy heart.) From the assumptions (1) that some motivation *M* that agents have for doing something *A* results in their doing *A* and (2) that they are aware that they have this motivation for doing *A*, it does not follow that they believe, consciously or otherwise, that they *are* doing *A* (in this case, purposely shifting their tolerance). Nor, a fortiori, does it follow that they believe, consciously or otherwise, that they are doing *A* for reasons having to do with *M*. They may falsely believe that *M* has no influence whatever on their behavior, while not possessing the contrary belief.

The following case illustrates both points. Ann, who consciously desires her parents' love, believes they would love her if she were a successful lawyer. Consequently, she enrolls in law school; in enrolling she is trying, unconsciously, to please her parents. But Ann does not believe, at any level, that in enrolling in law school she is trying to please her parents. Nor does she believe that her desire for her parents' love is in any way responsible for her decision to enroll. Ann believes she is enrolling solely because of an independent desire to become a lawyer. Of course, I have simply *stipulated* that Ann lacks the beliefs in question. But my point is that this stipulation does not render the scenario incoherent. My claim about the sincere deniers in

Quattrone and Tversky's study is that, similarly, there is no explanatory need to suppose they believe, at any level, that they are trying to shift their tolerance for diagnostic purposes, or even believe that they are trying to shift their tolerance at all. These subjects have motivation to generate favorable diagnostic evidence and they believe (to some degree) that a suitable change in their tolerance on the second trial would constitute such evidence. *But the motivation and belief can result in purposeful action independently of their believing, consciously or otherwise*, that they are "purposefully engaged in the behavior," or purposefully engaged in it "to make a favorable diagnosis."[9]

As Quattrone and Tversky's study indicates, people sometimes do not consciously recognize why they are doing what they are doing—for example, why they are now reporting a certain pain rating. Given that an *unconscious* recognition or belief that they are "purposefully engaged in the behavior to make a favorable diagnosis" in no way helps to account for the sincere deniers' behavior, why suppose that such recognition or belief is present? If one thought that normal adult human beings always recognize—at least at some level—what is motivating their behavior, one would opt for Quattrone and Tversky's dual-belief hypothesis about the sincere deniers. But Quattrone and Tversky offer no defense of the general thesis just mentioned. In light of their results, a convincing defense of that thesis would demonstrate that whenever such adults do not consciously recognize what they are up to, they nevertheless correctly believe that they are up to *x*, albeit without being aware that they believe this. That is a tall order.

Quattrone and Tversky suspect that (many of) the sincere deniers are *self-deceived* in believing that they did not try to shift their tolerance. They adopt Sackeim and Gur's analysis of self-deception (1984, p. 239) and interpret their results accordingly. However, an interpretation of their data that avoids the dual-belief assumption just criticized and assumes, with Quattrone and Tversky, that the subjects were trying to shift their tolerance allows for self-deception on a less demanding conception. One can hold (1) that sincere deniers, due partly to a desire to live a long, healthy life, had motivation to believe that they had a healthy heart; (2) that this motivation (in conjunction with a belief that an upward-downward shift in tolerance would constitute evidence for the favored proposition) led them to try to shift their tolerance; and (3) that this motivation also led them to believe that they were not purposely shifting their tolerance (and not to believe the opposite). Their motivated, false beliefs that they were not trying to alter their displayed tolerance can count as beliefs that they are self-deceived in holding without their *also* believing that they were attempting to do this.[10]

How did the subjects' motivation lead them to believe that they did not try to shift their tolerance (a belief that I am currently assuming to be false for argument's sake)? Quattrone and Tversky offer a suggestion (p. 243): "The physiological mechanism of pain may have facilitated self-deception in this experiment. Most people believe that heart responses and pain thresholds are ordinarily not under an individual's voluntary control. This widespread belief would protect the assertion that the shift could not have been on purpose, for how does one 'pull the strings'?" And notice that a belief that one did not try to alter the amount of time one left one's hand in the water before reporting a pain rating of "intolerable," one based (in part) upon a belief about ordinary uncontrollability of "heart responses and pain thresholds," need not be completely cold or unmotivated. Some subjects' motivation might render the "uncontrollability" belief very salient, for example, while also diverting attention from internal cues that they were trying to shift their tolerance, including the intensity of the pain. Furthermore, owing to relevant desires, the sincere deniers may be expected to have significantly higher confidence thresholds for acceptance of the hypothesis that they are trying to shift their tolerance than for rejection of that hypothesis.

Incidentally, like Quattrone and Tversky, biologist Robert Trivers (1985, pp. 416–17) endorses Gur and Sackeim's definition of self-deception and claims to find convincing evidence for self-deception, so conceived. Trivers maintains that self-deception has "evolved . . . because natural selection favors ever subtler ways of deceiving others" (p. 282; cf. pp. 415–20). We recognize that "shifty eyes, sweaty palms, and croaky voices may indicate the stress that accompanies conscious knowledge of attempted deception. By becoming unconscious of its deception, the deceiver hides these signs from the observer. He or she can lie without the nervousness that accompanies deception" (pp. 415–16). Trivers's thesis cannot adequately be assessed here, but the point should be made that the thesis in no way depends for its plausibility on self-deception's requiring the presence of beliefs whose propositional contents are mutually contradictory. Self-deception that satisfies the set of sufficient conditions I offered in Chapter 3 without satisfying the dual-belief requirement is no less effective a tool for deceiving others. Trivers's proposal hinges on the idea that agents who do not consciously believe the truth (*p*) have an advantage over agents who do in getting others to believe the pertinent falsehood (~*p*); consciousness of the truth tends to manifest itself in ways that tip one's hand. But notice that an *unconscious* belief that *p* provides no help at all in this connection. Furthermore, such a belief might generate telltale physiological signs of deception (recall the physiological manifestations of the alleged unconscious beliefs in Gur and Sackeim's studies). If unconscious true beliefs would make self-deceivers less subtle interpersonal deceivers than they would be without these beliefs, and if self-deception evolved because natural selection favors subtlety in the deception of others, better that it evolve on my model than on the "dual-belief" model Trivers accepts.

5. Did Quattrone and Tversky's Sincere Deniers Try to Shift Their Tolerance?

Thus far, I have assumed, for the sake of argument, that the relevant subjects were trying to shift their tolerance in order "to make a favorable diagnosis" and I have argued that, even so, we lack good reason to suppose that they believed that they were trying to shift their tolerance while also believing that they were not trying to shift it. In the present section, I attack Quattrone and Tversky's claim that the subjects were, in fact, trying to do this.

Recall the FTL model of everyday hypothesis testing, described in Chapter 2. Presumably, Quattrone and Tversky's subjects preferred having a healthy heart to having an unhealthy one, and it is plausible that the cost, in the FTL sense, of falsely believing that they had unhealthy hearts (substantial psychological distress) was considerably higher, under the circumstances, for many of them than the cost of falsely believing that their hearts were healthy.[11] Thus (factoring in information costs), one would expect that many subjects had much higher confidence thresholds for believing that their hearts were unhealthy than for believing that their hearts were healthy.

Consider a representative subject during the second trial. He finds himself faced with the question whether the pain he is now experiencing is intolerable. If he has been led to believe that increased tolerance is diagnostic of a healthy heart, then he may well have a higher confidence threshold for believing that his present pain is intolerable than for believing that it is tolerable.[12] Now, the notion of *intolerable* pain certainly is not a precise one, and when a person's pain is gradually increasing, it is far from obvious to the person at what point the pain has first become intolerable. Given this observation and assuming the difference in the confidence thresholds just mentioned, one would expect the subject to take longer this time to come to the belief that his pain is intolerable. And if, as is to be expected, the subject is testing the desirable hypothesis that his present pain is tolerable, then given the points about the imprecision and phenomenology of intolerability of pain, we should not be surprised to discover a common element of the confirmation bias—namely, the subject's interpreting "ambiguous" data as supporting the hypothesis being tested.[13] Similarly, on the FTL model, one would expect many subjects led to accept that *decreased* tolerance is indicative of a healthy heart to test the hypothesis that their present pain is intolerable and to come to the belief that their pain is intolerable sooner the second time around. In neither case is there an evident need, in explaining the data, to hold that these subjects were *trying* to bring it about that they believed certain things. Given that there is no clear first moment at which gradually increasing pain has become intolerable, and given the postulated confidence thresholds, such an exercise of agency is not required to explain the variation in pain ratings across trials.

Quattrone and Tversky's experiment produces powerful evidence that many of the subjects had motivationally biased beliefs about the intensity of their pain on the second trial. However, the evidence that these subjects were *trying* to shift their tolerance in an effort to produce or sustain a belief in the health of their hearts is quite weak. Their motivated beliefs are accommodated by the FTL model without postulating such exercises of agency.[14]

6. Conclusion

In criticizing attempted empirical demonstrations of the existence of self-deception on Sackeim and Gur's agency model without producing empirical evidence that the subjects do *not* have "two contradictory beliefs," have I been unfair to the researchers? Recall the dialectical situation. The researchers claim that they have demonstrated the existence of self-deception on the model at issue. I have shown that they have not demonstrated this. The tests they employ for the existence of "two contradictory beliefs" in their subjects are, for the reasons offered, inadequate. I have no wish to claim that it is impossible for an agent to believe that *p* while also believing that *~p*. My claim is that there is no explanatory need to postulate such beliefs either in familiar cases of self-deception or in the alleged cases cited by these researchers and that plausible alternative explanations of the data may be generated by appealing to mechanisms and processes that are relatively well understood.

I have not claimed that believing that *p* while also believing that *~p* is conceptually or psychologically impossible. But I have not encountered a compelling illustration of that phenomenon in a case of self-deception. Some readers may be inclined to suggest that illustrations may be found in the literature on multiple personality. However, that phenomenon, if it is a genuine one, raises thorny questions about the *self* in self-deception. In such alleged cases, do individuals deceive *themselves*, with the result that they believe that *p* while also believing that *~p*? Or do we rather have interpersonal deception—or, at any rate, something more closely resembling that than self-deception?[15] These are questions for another occasion. They take us far from ordinary self-deception.

Do I have a bias against agency views of self-deception? Perhaps, but I think not. I am happy to grant that there is a lot of unconscious processing of information (e.g., in perception). However, the proposition granted certainly does not entail that there is a lot of unconscious intentional action—for example, unconscious attempts to deceive ourselves, or to cause ourselves to believe certain things, or to make it easier for ourselves to believe these things. Nor does it entail that there are *any* such unconscious efforts. There is considerable evidence for the existence of the processes and phenomena that I have appealed to in developing the position I am offering on the explanation of garden-variety straight self-deception, a position that accounts for such self-deception without appealing to unconscious efforts of the kind mentioned, and it is fair to say that there is nothing approaching comparably weighty evidence for the occurrence of these unconscious efforts. We can explain representative instances of garden-variety straight self-deception, including cases as extreme as Gimpel's (ch. 3, sec. 4), without appealing to hidden efforts of these kinds, and because evidence that such efforts occur is, at best, very weak, I am strongly inclined to eschew appealing to them in an account of such self-deception. For the reasons just offered, this inclination does not appear to be a bias.

I conclude by reissuing a challenge that I mentioned at the beginning of this chapter. I challenge readers inclined to think that there are cases of self-deception in which the self-deceiver simultaneously believes that *p* and believes that ~*p* to provide convincing evidence of the existence of such self-deception. The most influential empirical work on the topic has not met the challenge, as I have shown. Perhaps some readers can do better. However, if my arguments in the preceding two chapters are on target, such cases will be *exceptional* instances of self-deception and not the norm.

5

Twisted Self-Deception

In what I have called "straight" self-deception, people are self-deceived in believing something they want to be true. Philosophical and psychological work on self-deception has focused on this phenomenon. Apparently, there also is a theoretically more perplexing, if much less common, kind of self-deception—a "twisted" kind. As I mentioned in Chapter 1, it might be exemplified by an insecure, jealous husband who believes that his wife is having an affair despite his possessing only relatively flimsy evidence for that proposition and despite his wanting it to be false that she is so engaged (and not also wanting it to be true).

Although the question how instances of twisted self-deception are to be explained is largely an empirical one, some philosophical headway may be made. Here, drawing partly on empirical literature, I develop a pair of approaches to explaining twisted self-deception: a motivation-centered approach, and a hybrid approach featuring both motivation and emotion. My aim is to display our resources for exploring and explaining twisted self-deception and to show that promising approaches are consistent with the position I have advanced on straight self-deception.

One critic has suggested that because my explanation of straight self-deception does not also explain the twisted kind, it is "a weak contender for accounting for self-deception" of any sort (Lazar 1997, p. 120). This might seem plausible, on the assumption that all instances of self-deception are to be explained in the same way. The suggestion is unpersuasive, however, even if the assumption is granted, as will become evident in section 2. Whether twisted and straight instances of self-deception are properly given an explanation of the same kind is among the questions addressed here.

1. Pears's Motivational Account

By definition, in *twisted* instances, people who are self-deceived in believing that *p* do not desire that *p*. This leaves it open, however, that their beliefs that *p* are motivated by some other desire. Indeed, one may think that if the pertinent beliefs are unmotivated, they either are inexplicable or are explicable only in ways that are inconsistent with a diagnosis of self-deception.

David Pears (1984), who understands self-deception on the model of interpersonal deception, offers a motivational explanation of the insecure, jealous husband's acquiring the false, unwarranted belief that his wife is having an affair despite his wanting it to be the case that she is innocent of the charge. He suggests both that the man wishes to "eliminat[e] all rivals" for his wife's affection and (without supposing that the husband is consciously thinking along these lines) that the value of his jealousy-inspired belief in his wife's infidelity lies in its capacity, in combination with his desire for her fidelity, to lead him to take steps to reduce the chance that she will have affairs by, for example, increasing his vigilance (1984, pp. 42–44). If Pears is right, the man is (unconsciously) motivationally attracted to believing that his wife is unfaithful because of the role that belief can play in his eliminating rivals, and this motivational attraction helps to explain why he acquires the belief.

Generalizing from Pears's diagnosis of this case, we get the following partial account: in twisted cases of *S*'s being self-deceived in believing that *p*, *S* desires that ~*p* and desires something, *x*, associated with ~*p* but is motivated to believe that *p* because so believing is conducive to *S*'s bringing about *x*. Of course, even if some instances of twisted self-deception are explicable along these lines, one is entitled to wonder whether all, or most, or many are; and even in the scenario that Pears selects, his proposal is questionable. Acquiring a belief that one's spouse is having an affair clearly is not the only route to increased vigilance concerning one's spouse's extramarital activities and to associated preventative measures; the belief that there is *evidence* that one's spouse is having an affair might be enough to turn the trick in a jealous person. Furthermore, if people sometimes are involved in twisted self-deception in underestimating their own abilities, talents, moral character, intelligence, attractiveness, and the like, efforts to explain this by postulating specific desires whose satisfaction is promoted by these underestimations may seem even more questionable (see Knight 1988, pp. 182–84). To be sure, it is possible that some such people have, for example, an especially acute fear of failure and that their underestimations reduce the chance that they will try to tackle difficult tasks, thereby promoting satisfaction of a desire to avoid failure. But convincing evidence that twisted self-deception is always properly given explanations of this kind is not available.

2. A Global Motivational Account

Implicit in the FTL model of everyday hypothesis testing (see ch. 2, sec. 2) is an interesting motivational diagnosis of what transpires in twisted self-deception, and one need not accept the model in its full generality to glean from it a partial basis for a potential explanation of this phenomenon. Recall that the "cost" of an error for an individual, in the FTL model, depends on the individual's interests and desires. Whereas for many people, perhaps, it may be more important to avoid acquiring the false belief that their spouses are having affairs than to avoid acquiring the false belief that they are not so engaged, the converse may well be true of some insecure, jealous people. The belief that one's spouse is unfaithful tends to cause significant psychological discomfort.[1] Even so, avoiding falsely believing that their spouses are faithful may be so important to some people that they test the relevant hypothesis in ways that are less likely to lead to a false belief in their spouses' fidelity than to a false belief in their spouses' infidelity. Furthermore, data suggestive of infidelity may be particularly salient for these people and contrary data quite pallid by comparison.

Why would anyone be in the psychological condition just described? Recall Pears's suggestion that the jealous man's false, unwarranted belief in his wife's infidelity is motivated by a desire to eliminate rivals for his wife's affection. Don Sharpsteen and Lee Kirkpatrick observe that "the jealousy complex" can be regarded as a mechanism "for maintaining close relationships" and that it appears to be "triggered by separation, or the threat of separation, from attachment figures" (1997, p. 627). It certainly is conceivable that, given a certain psychological profile, a strong desire to maintain one's relationship with one's spouse plays a role in rendering the potential error of falsely believing one's spouse to be innocent of infidelity a "costly" error, in the FTL sense, and more costly than the error of falsely believing one's spouse to be guilty of infidelity. After all, the former error may reduce the probability that one takes steps to protect the relationship against an intruder. (Pears's speculations about twisted self-deception may be regarded as complementing the account implicit in the FTL model by providing hypotheses about what makes relevant potential errors costly for agents.)

The FTL analysis of lay hypothesis testing suggests a "unifying" view of self-deception—specifically, the view that, in all cases of self-deception, straight and twisted alike, a tendency to minimize errors that are costly, given the person's current motivational profile, plays a central explanatory role. The FTL model supports my own position on straight self-deception, as I explain in previous chapters. But is it likely that the phenomena central to the FTL model are at work in *all* instances of self-deception? That is a difficult question. The correct answer depends, among other things, on the strength of the evidence for the truth of the FTL hypothesis and on the merits of alternative approaches to explaining self-deception. I turn now to one of the alternatives.

3. A Purely Emotional Account

In ordinary instances of straight self-deception, as I understand the phenomenon, at least part of what happens is that a desire that *p* makes it easier for the person to believe that *p* by leading to increased vividness of evidence for *p*, by enhancing the salience of various *p*-supporting memories of his, by prompting him to consider hypotheses supportive of *p* (thereby setting the stage for the confirmation bias), or the like. Sometimes these effects of a desire that *p* contribute to the acquisition or retention of an unwarranted, false belief that *p*.

If desires can do this, perhaps emotions can too.[2] In the absence of any desire for his wife's infidelity and any desire to believe that she is unfaithful, can our insecure man's jealousy regarding his wife render his apparent evidence that she is having an affair significantly more vivid than it would otherwise be, and render his competing evidence pallid by comparison? Can his jealousy lead him to focus his attention on rare memories of a seemingly flirtatious or secretive wife at the expense of attention to competing memories that an impartial spectator would regard as much more telling? Might he entertain the hypothesis that his wife is having an affair largely because he is jealous, thus unintentionally setting the stage for an operation of the confirmation bias that increases the probability of his believing her to be unfaithful?

There is empirical evidence that emotions can operate in these ways.[3] For example, as Douglas Derryberry observes, there is evidence that "emotional states facilitate the processing of congruent stimuli" and that "attentional processes are involved in [this] effect" (1988, pp. 36, 38).[4] Jealousy of one's spouse might render one more attentive, for instance, to memories of the sort I mentioned. And there is a philosophical precedent for finding the result that Derryberry reports unsurprising. Ronald de Sousa has argued that emotions enable us to circumvent the paralysis of informational overload by influencing (in his shorthand) the "salience" of our data. He writes: "For a variable but always limited time, an emotion limits the range of information that the organism will take into account, the inferences actually drawn from a potential infinity, and the set of live options among which it will choose" (1987, p. 195). Although de Sousa views this as the chief functional contribution of emotion to rational life, he admits that it may also backfire (e.g., p. 198).

Perhaps emotions play roles in twisted self-deception that parallel some of the roles I attributed to desire in straight self-deception. I dub the idea that they do this and that twisted self-deception has no desires as significant causes "hypothesis *E*." (Later I will consider a less stringent emotional hypothesis about twisted self-deception.)

Theorists attracted to the idea that all instances of self-deception are subject to the same general kind of explanation may look for unity where hypothesis *E* seems to urge diversity. Whereas Pears represents desire (motivation) as essential to self-deception of both the twisted and the straight varieties, others may search for a way of making emotion central (see Lazar 1999). Perhaps, for example, in straight cases of self-deception that *p*, it is not a mere desire that *p* that plays a central explanatory role, but rather a *fear* that ~*p*.[5] Indeed, this may be regarded by some proponents of the desire-emphasizing position about straight self-deception as a friendly amplification of their explanatory tack, because fear that ~*p* is plausibly understood as being partly constituted by desire that *p*.[6] It may also be suggested that an aversion to the fear that ~*p* or to the associated feeling of anxiety contributes to straight self-deception. Straight self-deception might often serve the purpose of reducing fear or anxiety.[7]

This attempt to achieve unity by postulating a common explanatory ingredient highlights a question that would arise in any case. Our jealous man wants it to be true that his wife is not having an affair, and presumably at some point he fears that she is so engaged. Why does his jealousy lead to a belief that she is unfaithful rather than his fear (or desire) leading to a belief that she is faithful? If his jealousy affected his attention, his framing of hypotheses, or the salience of his evidence in a way that contributed to his acquiring a belief that his wife is unfaithful, why did it not happen instead that his fear—or his desire that she not be having an affair—affected these things in a way that contributed to his acquiring a belief that she is faithful? Alternatively, why didn't his fear block the relevant potential effects of his jealousy, with the result that his evidence carried the day?

These are difficult questions. Answers that properly inspire confidence will not, I fear, be produced by philosophical speculation. Nor are such answers available in the empirical literature on emotion: we need to know more than is currently known about the effects of emotions on cognition. But these observations do not themselves quash hypothesis *E*. They leave it open that in some, or even all, instances of twisted self-deception emotion plays a major explanatory role, even without the assistance of desires.

A theorist might consider putting the FTL model to work in answering the questions just raised in a way unfavorable to the emotional account. In a typical case of romantic jealousy where there are some grounds for suspecting infidelity, the belief that one's romantic partner is having an affair presumably would cause psychological discomfort, but it might *also* promote one's chances of taking successful steps to save one's relationship. It may be suggested (1) that what the agent ends up believing is determined by a combination of (*a*) the strength of his evidence for and against the proposition that his partner is having an affair and (*b*) which error he has the strongest motivation to avoid and (2) that *b* is determined by the relative strengths of his aversion to the psychological discomfort of believing that his partner is having an affair and of his desire to maintain the relationship. This view of things, however, may be too simple. Perhaps distinctively emotional features of jealousy can influence what the agent believes in a way that does not depend on desire (motivation). Furthermore, even if desire and desire-strength are relevant to what the agent comes to believe, that relevance is consistent with the truth of a modified version of the emotional account that accords both emotion and motivation a role in explaining some cases of twisted self-deception. I explore a modified account of this kind in section 6.

One may wonder whether a phenomenon that is explained by emotion in the way suggested by hypothesis *E* can properly count as self-deception. If our jealous man believes that his wife is unfaithful because of the effects of his jealousy on the salience of his evidence or on the focus of his attention, has he deceived himself, or has he simply been taken in by processes beyond his control? Notice that a parallel question can be raised about false, unwarranted beliefs that *p* that are prompted by desires that *p* in the ways I described in Chapters 2 and 3. But if some of the examples I offered in that connection are properly regarded as instances of *self-deception* even if the false, unwarranted beliefs are produced in the way I suggested they are, the operation of the relevant processes themselves in the production of a belief does not preclude the acquisition of that belief's being an instance of self-deception. If the present question poses a challenge that is specific to hypothesis *E*, therefore, the worry apparently hinges on the particular emotional triggers and sustainers of the relevant processes, not on the processes themselves. It may be thought, for example, that although we (often or sometimes) are not helpless regarding the effects of our desires that *p* on what we believe about *p*, we are helpless regarding what we believe about *p* when possessed of the *emotions* that allegedly result in twisted self-deception about *p*.

Is this right? It should be observed that we have some control over what emotions we have at a given time and over the intensity of our emotions.[8] We stem a discomforting flow of pity for characters in a film by reminding ourselves that they are *only* characters (cf. Koriat, Melkman, Averill, and Lazarus 1972, pp. 613, 617). The woman who regards her anger at her child as unacceptable may dissolve or attenuate it by forcing herself to focus her thoughts on a cherished moment with the child. The timid employee who believes that he can muster the courage to demand a raise only if he becomes angry at his boss may deliberately make himself angry by vividly representing injustices he has suffered at the office (cf. Skinner 1953, p. 236; Tice and Baumeister 1993, pp. 401–2). These are instances of *internal* control over one's emotions. Many emotions and feelings are subject to *external* control as well—control through one's overt behavior. Jill knows that if, for some reason, she wants to be angry, a phone call to her mother will turn the trick. Jack defeats mild depression by calling his sister.

There is a lively debate in social psychology about the extent to which sources of biased belief are subject to our control.[9] There also is evidence that some prominent sources of bias are to some degree controllable. For example, people can reduce the effects of bias "simply by trying harder to gather more information" (Baumeister and Newman 1994, p. 7), subjects instructed to conduct "symmetrical memory searches" are less likely than others to fall prey to the confirmation bias, and subjects' confidence in their responses to "knowledge questions" is reduced when they are invited to provide grounds for doubting the correctness of those responses (Kunda 1990, pp. 494–95). Presumably, people aware of the confirmation bias may reduce biased thinking in themselves by *giving themselves* the former instruction; and we sometimes remind ourselves to consider both the pros *and* the cons before making up our minds about the truth of important propositions—even when we are tempted to do otherwise. The *extent* of our self-control regarding what we believe is an empirical issue in need of further empirical investigation. That we do have some control over the influence of emotions and motivation on our beliefs is, however, indisputable; and that control is a resource for combating self-deception.

It would be rash, then, to assume that our jealous man's jealousy ineluctably results in his believing that his wife is unfaithful. As I observed elsewhere, jealousy need not turn an agent into an automaton (Mele 1987a, p. 117). A jealous man may know that he is disposed to make unwarranted inferences regarding his wife's fidelity and attempt to prevent this from happening when he finds himself entertaining relevant suspicions. He might try to exercise self-control by seeking reassurance from his wife, or by relating to friends his suspicion and the flimsy grounds on which it rests, with a view to generating salient support for the fidelity hypothesis. At any rate, whether hypothesis *E* is in fact true or false, it cannot plausibly be argued to be false on the grounds that in no alleged case of emotional twisted self-deception was it in the person's power to take reasonable measures such that, if they had been taken, self-deception would have been avoided. Hypothesis *E* is still in the running, and even if some instances of twisted self-deception are explained (partly) by motivation, as on the FTL model, others might be explained instead by emotion.

4. A Purely Cognitive Account and Its Shortcomings

Martha Knight (1988), responding to *Irrationality* (Mele 1987a), offers a cognitive account of some alleged cases of twisted self-deception that parallels my own motivational account of straight self-deception and the emotional account of twisted self-deception. Knight discusses a pair of examples.[10] One features the formation and persistence of an unwarranted, distressing belief that one is personally responsible for a tragic event (p. 182). The other is a textbook case of chronic self-underestimation associated with low self-esteem (p. 183).

Knight discusses a mother (mentioned in Chodoff, Friedman, and Hamburg 1964) who blamed herself for her child's dying of leukemia (p. 182). Despite a doctor's "attempts to dissuade her," the mother persisted in believing that "her daughter 'caught' leukemia from tumors on a family pet" and that she could have prevented her daughter's illness by removing the pet from their house. Knight considers and rejects a pair of motivational explanations of the formation and persistence of the distressing belief: the mother "unconsciously wanted to try to increase her sense of control in order to convince herself that harmful events can be avoided if proper action is taken"; she "wanted to punish herself for some past transgression." She is skeptical about the merits of motivational explanations of any kind in this scenario.

In the case of self-underestimation, Knight explicitly argues for a cognitive explanation. She writes:

> The structure of one's self-schema can, in part, produce selective attention to information relevant to the schema, organisation of that information into categories already found in the self-schema, and, as a result, selective recall of schema-relevant information. . . . In particular, schema consistent information is particularly likely to be noticed, processed, and recalled, while information inconsistent with or irrelevant to one's self-schema is likely to be overlooked, or if noticed, processed less deeply, and recalled less well. (p. 183)

And she contends that a typical chronic self-underestimator's unwarranted relevant negative beliefs about herself are unmotivated: "this example seems much better explained by a perceptual/cognitive explanation . . . than by a motivational one" (p. 183).

If, as Knight suggests, the relevant beliefs in both cases are best given a purely "perceptual/cognitive explanation," is either plausibly regarded as a case of self-deception? Again, to say that someone is *deceived* in believing that *p*, in one use of the term, is simply to say that what he believes is false. People who cause themselves to have false beliefs—and, therefore, to be deceived in this sense—need not be guilty of self-deception. Here is a simple illustration. Al is relatively competent at arithmetic, he knows that he sometimes makes arithmetical mistakes, and he is able to avoid many mistakes by double checking. Just now, while helping his daughter with her homework, he accidentally added a long column of numbers improperly and, without double checking, wrote down the figure at which he arrived. Al has caused himself to have a false belief about the sum. Unless there is more to the story, however, a charge of self-deception is outlandish. Self-deception is more than just self-caused false belief.

Al's acquiring his false belief about the sum is best given a purely "perceptual/cognitive explanation" and it is not a case of self-deception. Should we think that matters are different in Knight's cases? Of course, we might think that the best explanation of what happens in her cases is *not* purely "perceptual/cognitive" and that these cases do involve self-deception. (Chodoff et al. [1964, pp. 746–47] offer a motivational explanation of the mother's belief. I comment briefly on it later.) But suppose we were to discover that the first conjunct of this conjunctive thought is false. Should we still embrace the second conjunct? Knight argues that we should:

> A person who is generally aware that his/her social judgments might be unduly biased by perceptual/cognitive processes, may be able to exert considerable control over them. . . . Potentially, then, some people are capable of the type of control that would allow them to examine and control their cognitive strategies. If instead they persist in using biased strategies to search for, combine, and retrieve information, with the consequences that their biased cognitive strategies lead them to draw false conclusions about the truth of *p*, we would say that their false belief is the result of self-deception. (1988, p. 186)

She contends as well that when people persist "in using cognitive strategies which they should know are biased, . . . they are . . . self-deceived, ignorant, and responsible for that ignorance if those cognitive strategies result in false belief" (p. 185).[11]

As self-deception is commonly conceived, if *S* is self-deceived in believing that *p*, and *D* is the collection of relevant data readily available to *S*, then if *D* were made readily available to *S*'s impartial cognitive peers (including merely hypothetical people), those who conclude that *p* is false would significantly outnumber those who conclude that *p* is true. Call this "the impartial-observer test." Cognitive peers who share certain relevant desires with *S*—as one's spouse may share one's desire that one's child is not seriously ill or that the child is not experimenting with drugs—may often acquire the same unwarranted belief that *S* does, given the same data. But, again, the relevant cognitive peers, for present purposes, are *impartial* observers. At least a minimal requirement for impartiality in the present context is that one neither shares *S*'s desire that *p* nor has a desire that ~*p*. Another plausible requirement for impartiality is that one not prefer avoidance of either of the following errors over the other: falsely believing that *p* and falsely believing that ~*p*. I take the appropriateness of the impartial observer test to be implicit in the conceptual framework that informs commonsense judgments about what is and is not plausibly construed as an example of self-deception.[12]

Assume that the mother (I call her Dolores) whose daughter died of leukemia "is generally aware that [her] social judgments might be unduly biased by perceptual/cognitive processes." Assume as well that Dolores's distressing belief is to be given a purely "perceptual/cognitive explanation." And consider the following story about her. Dolores knows that the family cat was diagnosed with leukemia some time before her daughter was. Later, a neighbor tells her about another case in which a child is diagnosed with leukemia not long after the family cat is. Dolores, a woman of average intelligence with a high school education, now has a hypothesis about her own daughter's death. She asks relatives, friends, and neighbors whether they know of any cases in which a family pet's being diagnosed with leukemia precedes a family member's being diagnosed with the same illness, and she hears of a few additional such cases. Dolores concludes that her daughter's leukemia was caused by contact with her sick cat, and she is utterly unimpressed by the physician's attempts to dissuade her. She lacks confidence in him and in the medical community in general: after all, they failed to save her daughter.

Dolores is guilty of shoddy reasoning, but as the story stands, if her belief is to be given a purely "perceptual/cognitive explanation," a charge of self-deception is difficult to sustain. Probably, many of Dolores's impartial cognitive peers would arrive at the same conclusion she did when presented with her evidence. *They* would not count as self-deceived. This indicates that Dolores is not self-deceived either, given that the explanation of her belief, like theirs, is of a strictly "perceptual/cognitive" kind.

What about Knight's self-underestimator, Susan? Because Susan's self-schema is a purely "perceptual/cognitive" matter, her hypothetical cognitive peers will share it, in the sense that their Susan-schema will match her self-schema. Suppose that the data available to Susan were made available to her impartial cognitive peers. What would these observers believe about Susan's abilities, accomplishments, and the like—if as Knight claims, Susan's self-underestimations are properly given a purely "perceptual/cognitive explanation"? Pretty much the same things that Susan herself believes, one suspects. After all, schema-produced effects on attention, organization, recall, and so on that occur in Susan are likely to occur as well in these hypothetical peers. (If Susan's self-schema were assumed to have an important nonperceptual, noncognitive dimension, all bets would be off. But then the beliefs that Susan allegedly is self-deceived in holding would not be explained in a purely "perceptual/cognitive" way.) That Susan's relevant peers would tend to agree with her is a significant indication that her unmotivated self-underestimations are not instances of self-deception. Impartial observers of the kind imagined presumably would not be self-deceived in coming to the conclusions they do. That indicates that Susan is not self-deceived in coming to the same conclusions.

If Susan's characteristic self-underestimations are to be given a purely "perceptual/cognitive explanation," then the presence of the self-schema that Knight assigns a leading role in explaining Susan's self-underestimations presumably is itself to be given a nonmotivational, nonemotional explanation. If motivation or emotion plays a role in accounting for Susan's self-schema, it might well play a role in accounting for her self-underestimations. Now, Susan is seriously mistaken about herself, and we may suppose that she has the capacity to revise her offending self-schema. But if her self-schema and her related false beliefs about herself are to be given a wholly "perceptual/cognitive explanation," how is the (unexercised) control that she is capable of exerting over her "perceptual/cognitive processes" any more supportive of a charge of self-deception than is the (unexercised) control that Al could have exerted over the process that leads to his false arithmetical belief? Perhaps, as Knight suggests, Susan can be held responsible for not critically examining and modifying her self-schema, even though her not doing so is not even partly explained by motivational or emotional factors. But that does not render her self-deceived in holding the false, schema-inspired beliefs that she does. If it did, Al would be self-deceived in holding his false, addition-inspired arithmetical belief: if Susan can be held responsible for the omission identified, Al can be held responsible for his failure to double-check his addition. And, again, Al plainly is not self-deceived in believing what he does about the arithmetic problem.

Earlier, I claimed that the appropriateness of the impartial observer test is implicit in the conceptual framework that informs commonsense judgments about what does or does not count as an instance of self-deception. A strand of thought in the preceding few paragraphs supports this claim. *Why* don't we count Dolores's and Susan's impartial cognitive peers as self-deceived? And why are we so confident that Al is not self-deceived in acquiring his arithmetical belief? A plausible answer is that we do not count these people as self-deceived because we see their beliefs as *impartially* acquired. This implies that we take relevant partiality to be required for entering self-deception in acquiring a belief. And if we are right about that, it is appropriate to test for satisfaction of a requirement for self-deception by asking whether the majority of *S*'s impartial cognitive peers (including merely hypothetical people) with the same information would acquire the same belief as *S*. If they would, that supports the claim that *S*, too, is impartial and therefore is not self-deceived. If they would acquire the contrary belief, we have grounds for holding that *S* satisfies at least one requirement for self-deception.

Readers may be inclined to see self-deception in the case of Dolores or Susan, and they may be importing ***motivational*** or ***emotional*** elements into the background of the stories. It is worth noting that given the ubiquity of motivation in lay hypothesis testing on Friedrich's PEDMIN view, proponents of that view would be committed to the idea that motivation is at work in these cases whether they are instances of self-deception or not. Naturally, one wonders what could explain Dolores's having stronger motivation to avoid falsely believing that she is not responsible for her daughter's death than to avoid falsely believing that she is responsible. After all, the former belief, whether true or false, would seem to be much more comforting. Similarly, one wonders why Susan would be more averse to overestimating her accomplishments and abilities than to underestimating them. There are stock answers. Perhaps, as Knight mentioned, it is especially important to Dolores that she not underestimate her ability to prevent tragic events. Or as Chodoff et al. contended, she might have had an "urgent need" for a "meaningful and understandable explanation" that undermines the personally unacceptable hypothesis that the "child had been stricken at random by a chance, impersonal blow" (1964, pp. 746–47); for some people, the "randomness" belief might be more painful than the "personal responsibility" belief. And perhaps Susan is particularly concerned not to set herself up for embarrassing falls by overestimating herself. However plausible or implausible these motivational hypotheses may be, if they are true in these cases, the women might be self-deceived. But if no (partly) motivational or emotional explanation of their false beliefs is correct, the two women seem no more self-deceived than Al does.

5. The Emotional Account Revisited

Even if Knight's attempted cognitive account of twisted self-deception presupposes an unduly inclusive conception of self-deception, my criticism of it prompts a significant question about the emotional position. If Dolores and Susan are not self-deceivers on the hypothesis that their relevant beliefs have a wholly "perceptual/cognitive explanation," why should they count as self-deceivers on the hypothesis that these beliefs have an emotional explanation of the kind sketched in section 3? There I criticized the claim that the emotional position fails because we have no prospects for controlling the influence of our emotions on what we believe. Knight argues, in effect, that we have comparable control over the influence of our self-schemas on our beliefs. Granting this, is there a crucial difference between the emotional and the "perceptual/cognitive" accounts of twisted self-deception in light of which we may reasonably accept the former view while reasonably rejecting the latter?

Recall the jealous husband. I suggested that his jealousy might increase the vividness of his apparent evidence that his wife is having an affair while also rendering his competing evidence more pallid than it would otherwise be, lead him to focus his attention on rare memories of a seemingly flirtatious or secretive wife at the expense of attention to competing memories that are more telling, or set the stage for an operation of the confirmation bias that increases the probability of his believing her to be unfaithful. On Knight's view, self-schemas can have the same effects. Suppose that a man, John, sees himself as the sort of person who is likely to be sexually betrayed by romantic partners, that this self-conception is unwarranted, and that it is not even partly explained by motivational or emotional factors. Given the same evidence about his wife that our jealous man has about his own wife, John may, owing to the effects of his self-schema on his evidence, acquire the false belief that his wife is having an affair—a belief that is properly given a purely "perceptual/cognitive explanation." If the two women Knight described are not self-deceived, on the assumption that she is right about the etiology of their false beliefs, then neither is John. But if John is not self-deceived, why should we think that his jealous counterpart is?

Return to what I called "the impartial-observer test." John's relevant impartial cognitive peers have the schema of John that he has of himself, including his conception of himself as the sort of person who is likely to be sexually betrayed by romantic partners. In short, their John-schema is his self-schema. What are they likely to conclude when given the additional relevant data possessed by John? As in Susan's case, they are likely to conclude whatever John concludes: after all, the same data are possessed by John and the others, they are cognitive peers, and John, like the others, is, by hypothesis, impartial. This indicates that John is not self-deceived in believing that his wife is having an affair, just as his imagined peers would not be self-deceived in believing this.

How is the case of John's emotional counterpart different? Apply the impartial observer test to this man, Jeff. Given the data possessed by Jeff, his belief that his wife is having an affair is unwarranted. His impartial cognitive peers who are given the same data are likely to see that this is so and to believe that Jeff's wife is not having an affair. So Jeff passes the test for the satisfaction of a necessary condition of self-deception that John fails, and a likely hypothesis about why he and his impartial peers do not agree is that Jeff's jealousy plays a role in biasing his thinking.

6. A Hybrid Motivational/Emotional Account

In the present section, I turn to the possibility of a hybrid motivational/emotional account of twisted self-deception. On the

FTL model, people tend to test hypotheses in ways that minimize "costly errors," and which errors are costly may be a function of relevant desires *and* emotions. A desire that *p*, given a certain psychological profile, may contribute to an agent's having stronger motivation to avoid falsely believing that ~*p* than to avoid falsely believing that *p*, which in turn may contribute to straight self-deception about *p*; and there is no reason to deny that an emotion like anxiety about *p* can play a role here. In *twisted* cases of being self-deceived in believing that *p*, on the FTL model, which errors are most costly for the agent hinges on desires, but not on a desire that *p*. For example, Dolores's case might centrally involve a desire for an explanation of her daughter's death that undermines the personally unacceptable hypothesis that the child "had been stricken at random by a chance, impersonal blow," and in Susan's case, a desire to minimize embarrassing failed attempts might play a major role. Dolores's motivation to avoid falsely believing that her daughter's death was a random occurrence might have been stronger than her motivation to avoid falsely believing that she herself was partly responsible for the death, and Susan might have had stronger motivation to avoid falsely believing that she is proficient in certain spheres than to avoid falsely believing that she is not proficient in those spheres. This is entirely consistent with emotion's having had a hand in the biasing. Perhaps it is not Dolores's desire alone that biases her thinking, but the desire together with her aversion to the *anxiety* she experiences when contemplating the "randomness" hypothesis as a candidate for belief. And perhaps Susan was biased by a complex motivational and emotional condition featuring anxiety about failure and the desire to avoid failure that that emotion involves.

According to hypothesis *E* (presented in section 3), emotion has biasing effects on cognition that *parallel* some biasing effects of motivation. Furthermore, hypothesis *E* denies that motivation has a significant role in producing twisted self-deception. In this connection, Tim Dalgleish writes: "it is inappropriate to suggest that jealous persons desire or are motivated to find that their partners are unfaithful; rather, their emotional state is priming the relevant processing systems to gather evidence in a biased fashion" (1997, p. 110). But what is included in this emotional state? Might it include relevant motivation?

A pair of psychologists mentioned earlier, Don Sharpsteen and Lee Kirkpatrick, suggest, plausibly, that "the jealousy complex"—that is, "the thoughts, feelings, and behavior typically associated with jealousy episodes" (1997, p. 627)—is "a manifestation of motives reflecting both sexual and attachment concerns" (p. 638). Jealousy is tightly bound up with *desires* (motivation) that jealous people have regarding their relationships with the people of whom they are jealous. It is a truism that if X is indifferent about his relationship with Y, X will not be jealous of Y.[13] (Being envious of someone is a distinct matter. For a useful discussion of the difference, see Farrell 1980, pp. 530–34.) Indeed, it is plausible that romantic jealousy is partly *constituted* by a desire for close romantic attachment to the relevant person, or, failing that, that such a desire is a significant part of the *cause* of such jealousy.[14] If that is right, then if Jeff's jealousy regarding his wife affects the focus of his attention, the vividness of his evidence, and the hypotheses he frames about his wife, it is a good bet that motivation has a hand in this. As I mentioned in section 2, Sharpsteen and Kirkpatrick observe that "the jealousy complex" can be regarded as a mechanism "for maintaining close relationships" and that it appears to be "triggered by separation, or the threat of separation, from attachment figures" (1997, p. 627). This suggests that the effects of jealousy are partly explained by a desire for the maintenance of a close relationship; that desire may be at work in Jeff's biased cognition. The desire, given its psychological context, including, importantly, the jealousy associated with it, may help enhance the salience of evidence of threats to the maintenance of Jeff's relationship with his wife, help prime the confirmation bias in a way favoring the belief that she is having an affair, and so on. To return to the FTL model, the desire, given the context mentioned, may contribute to Jeff's having stronger motivation to avoid falsely believing that his wife is faithful than to avoid falsely believing that she is unfaithful and, accordingly, contribute to his having a lower threshold for acceptance of the hypothesis that his wife is having an affair than for acceptance of the contrary hypothesis.

Owing to the tight connection between emotions and associated desires, testing empirically for cases of self-deception in which emotion, and not motivation, plays a biasing role promises to be difficult. Constructing compelling conceptual tests would also be challenging. For example, if all emotions, or all emotions that might plausibly bias beliefs, are partly constituted by desires, it would be difficult to show that there are beliefs that are biased by an emotion, or by some feature of an emotion, but not at all by desires, including desires that are constituents of the biasing emotions. Jealousy, as I explained, is plausibly regarded as having a desire as a constituent, or at least as a partial cause. The same is true, for example, of love, hate, fear, anxiety, ecstasy, envy, disgust, pride, sadness, grief, terror, anger, joy, and sorrow. It would be difficult to show that there are cases of self-deception in which one of these emotions plays a biasing role but no associated desire does. Even if there is a conceptual connection between types of emotions and types of motivational *causes*, rather than between types of emotions and types of motivational constituents, a case would have to be made that emotions sometimes contribute to instances of self-deception to which their motivational causes make no biasing contribution. Furthermore, even if an emotion can be found that is neither partially constituted nor partially caused by a desire (typical instances of surprise are like this), hypothesis *E* requires that its contribution to twisted self-deception not be causally mediated by a desire either and, more generally, that it not contribute to such self-deception in tandem with any biasing desire. Of course, hypothesis *E* requires as well that *no* cases of twisted self-deception have desires among their significant causes. The hypothesis plainly is excessive.

Hypothesis *E* should be distinguished from what may be termed "the direct emotion hypothesis," the hypothesis that emotions sometimes contribute *directly* to self-deception, including the twisted kind, in the following sense: they make contributions that, at the time, are neither made by desires nor causally mediated by desires. This hypothesis is consistent with the idea that motivation is at work in the production of all instances of twisted self-deception: perhaps emotions always make their direct contributions to such self-deception in conjunction with motivational causes. The hypothesis is consistent as well with the claim that emotion sometimes contributes to an instance of twisted self-deception that has no desires as significant causes.

It would be a mistake to lose sight of potential contributions of emotions to self-deception while emphasizing difficulties that face a proponent of hypothesis *E*. It may be that in some or many instances of self-deception, including the twisted variety, biasing roles are played both by emotions and by desires that are intimately related to the biasing emotions—either as part to whole, or as a partial cause or effect, or as responses to the emotions (as in the case of a desire to be rid of one's present anxiety). In some such cases, the biasing roles played by emotions may be "direct," in the sense just defined. Perhaps an emotion can prime the confirmation bias or enhance the salience of emotion-congruent data without doing so simply in virtue of a constituent desire's playing this role and without the effect's being causally mediated by a desire. For example, if Carl is angry at Dan for a recent offense, his anger might suggest an emotion-congruent hypothesis about Dan's current behavior (e.g., that Dan is behaving offensively), thereby priming the confirmation bias, and it might increase the salience of data that lend some support to that hypothesis. If anger has a desire as a constituent, it is, roughly, a desire to lash out against the target of one's anger. Possibly, anger can play the biasing roles just mentioned in its own right—rather than in virtue of this constituent desire's playing them, for example—and in a way that does not depend on causal mediation by a desire.[15]

Return to jealous Jeff. If we were to be made aware only of his relevant evidence and his desire for the maintenance of a close relationship with his wife and had no further information about him, we would not be well positioned to understand his believing that his wife is having an affair. Seemingly, people with much stronger evidence of infidelity—evidence that warrants an infidelity belief—often believe that their spouses are innocent of infidelity, even though they, like Jeff, strongly desire the maintenance of close relationships with their spouses. The information that Jeff is jealous helps us to get a grip on what might account for his infidelity belief. His jealousy is an important part of the psychological context in which the belief is acquired. It is plausible that Jeff's jealousy plays a role in the production of his biased belief that is not played by the pertinent desire alone.

If, as I suggested, an emotion can play a direct biasing role in self-deception, the door is open to the possibility that an emotion may contribute to an instance of self-deception that has *no* desires as significant causes. It is conceivable, perhaps, that Carl enters self-deception in acquiring the belief that Dan is behaving offensively now, that the process that results in this belief features his anger's playing the biasing roles I described, and that no desires of Carl's play a biasing role in this case. On the assumption that Carl believes that Dan is behaving offensively despite his having stronger evidence for the falsity of that hypothesis than for its truth, a proponent of the FTL model will find it quite natural to suppose that Carl had a lower threshold for acceptance of that hypothesis than for rejection of it, that the difference in thresholds is accounted for at least partly in terms of relevant desires, and that this difference helps to explain Carl's acquiring the belief he does. But this supposition is open to debate, and I will not try to settle the issue here. A hybrid motivational/emotional account of twisted self-deception, and of self-deception in general, that affirms the possibility of direct motivational biasing in the absence of motivational causes of the biased belief is in the running.

I will not try to settle here the potential dispute between a purely emotional account of some cases of twisted self-deception and a hybrid motivational/emotional view that attributes a biasing influence to a relevant desire in every case of twisted self-deception. Fortunately, given my purposes in this chapter, and in this book, I can afford to be open-minded both about the potential dispute just named and about disputes between hybrid accounts and strictly motivational accounts of some instances of twisted self-deception. Twisted self-deception is theoretically challenging, but it is not inexplicable. As I have shown, we have a variety of resources to draw on in exploring and explaining the phenomenon. Furthermore, the motivational and hybrid positions on twisted self-deception sketched here are entirely compatible with my own account of garden-variety straight self-deception.

6

Conclusion

In this book, I have been much more concerned with explanatory questions about self-deception than with conceptual questions about it. My focus has been the *explanation* of self-deception. Although I have offered a collection of jointly sufficient conditions for entering self-deception in acquiring a belief that *p* (ch. 3), I have not offered a statement of individually *necessary* and jointly sufficient conditions for this. My primary reason for having eschewed the latter task is that, given its difficult nature and constraints on space, a proper attempt to complete it would have changed the intended focus of this book. I am no foe of conceptual analysis, but, like the majority of the multidisciplinary audience that I have had in mind, I find the explanatory questions about self-deception more interesting. However, it may be appropriate now to say something about the general shape that a conceptual analysis of entering self-deception in acquiring a belief that *p* might take.

Obviously, an analysis of the notion just mentioned would not exhaust the conceptual subject matter. For example, entering self-deception in retaining a belief that *p* and remaining in self-deception in continuing to believe that *p* would also require attention. Analytical discussion of these notions must be reserved for another occasion.

1. Analyzing Self-Deception

The jointly sufficient conditions I offer for entering self-deception in acquiring a belief that *p*, again, are these:

1. The belief that *p* which *S* acquires is false.
2. *S* treats data relevant, or at least seemingly relevant, to the truth value of *p* in a motivationally biased way.
3. This biased treatment is a nondeviant cause of *S*'s acquiring the belief that *p*.
4. The body of data possessed by *S* at the time provides greater warrant for ~*p* than for *p*.

In Chapter 3, section 1, I explained why condition 1 should be regarded as a necessary condition and why condition 4 should not. Perhaps a suitably biased acquisition of a false belief that *p* is both necessary and sufficient for entering self-deception in acquiring a belief that *p*. If so, the analyst's chief task is to construct a correct account of *suitably biased* belief acquisition, that is, of belief acquisition that is biased in a way appropriate to self-deception. The task is challenging, indeed. Among other things, the analyst would need to produce an analysis of *biased* belief acquisition, handle problems posed by deviant causal chains, and tackle questions about *degrees* of bias.

The central question about degrees is straightforward. How biased must a process of belief-acquisition be if the resulting false belief is to count as "suitably" biased? It is highly unlikely that there will be a consensus about a precise specification of a degree-of-bias threshold in an analysis of self-deception. The ordinary concept of self-deception probably is vague on this dimension, as the ordinary concept of baldness is vague about the minimum degree of hair loss sufficient for baldness. In Chapter 5, I sketched what I called "the impartial-observer test"—a test for the satisfaction of a necessary condition of self-deception—and I suggested that the appropriateness of the test is underwritten by the ordinary concept of self-deception. The relevant complex conditional, again, is this: "if *S* is self-deceived in believing that *p*, and *D* is the collection of relevant data readily available to *S*, then if *D* were made readily available to *S*'s impartial cognitive peers (including merely hypothetical people), those who conclude that *p* is false would significantly outnumber those who conclude that *p* is true." This is a test for a kind of bias. In light of the discussion in which the test was featured (see ch. 5, secs. 4 and 5), the kind of bias at issue might broadly be termed "motivational or emotional bias." Although I have had a lot to say about biasing causes and processes, I have left it open that a *motivationally* biased treatment of data is not required for self-deception and that, in some cases, emotions do the biasing work without a desire's playing a biasing role. By what proportion must those who conclude that *p* is false outnumber those who conclude that *p* is true for the outnumbering to be significant? I doubt that the ordinary concept of self-deception yields a precise answer, but I do suggest that the notion of an impartial-observer test will prove useful in thinking both about degrees of bias involved in self-deception and about bias itself.

Deviant causal chains pose interesting problems in a variety of spheres for the project of providing causal analyses of concepts (e.g., the concepts of action, intentional action, memory, and perception). The project of providing a causal analysis of entering self-deception in acquiring a belief that *p* is no exception. It is important to understand, as background, that causal deviance is an interest-relative notion. Here is a simple illustration. Vera, who is skilled in the use of firearms, intends to hit a certain target. She takes careful aim at it and fires. Her aim, surprisingly, is seriously errant. More surprisingly, her bullet ricochets off of a stone wall and a metal pipe into the target.

From the point of view of physics, there is nothing strange or deviant about the causal sequence. But from the perspective of someone concerned to make judgments about intentional action, there is. Owing to the wayward causal chain linking Vera's intentional firing to the bullet's striking the target, we say that hitting the target is not something she did intentionally.

Consider the following adaptation of an example Robert Audi has discussed (1997, p. 104). Owing to his hoping that an airplane crash was caused by "mechanical failure" rather than by a terrorist act, Bob gathers evidence in a one-sided way. He seeks out people likely to favor the former causal hypothesis and avoids raising the issue with people likely to favor the latter. Among the people Bob approaches about the issue is Eva, a friend who has openly rejected a wide variety of terrorist hypotheses. As it happens, Eva believes that terrorists were at work on this occasion and that a terrorist bomb caused the crash. She convinces Bob that that is so, even though, in fact, the crash was caused by mechanical failure and the evidence readily available to Bob supports the true hypothesis more strongly than the false one.

Bob's approach to evidence-gathering in this case is motivationally biased. His biased approach led him to Eva, who convinced him that the crash was caused by a bomb. Consequently, his false belief that a bomb caused the crash was a product in part of his motivationally biased approach. Even so, other things being equal, Bob is not self-deceived in believing that the crash was caused by a bomb. But why not? What accounts for its being false that he is self-deceived about this, even though his belief was caused in part by his motivationally biased approach to evidence-gathering?

The short answer is that the route from Bob's motivationally biased evidence-gathering to his acquiring the pertinent belief is deviant. The biased process at issue does not result in Bob's false belief in a way appropriate to self-deception (just as Vera's intentional firing act does not result in the bullet's hitting the target in a way appropriate to her having intentionally hit the target). Bob's selective approach to evidence-gathering in this case—an instance of selectively gathering evidence for *p* owing to a desire that *p*—is an approach of a kind that contributes to self-deception, when it does, by leading one to overlook relatively easily obtainable evidence for ~*p* while finding less accessible evidence for *p*, thereby leading one to believe that *p* (ch. 2, sec. 1). His approach—again, an instance of selectively gathering evidence *for p motivated by a desire that p*—is of a kind that leads to self-deception by increasing the subjective probability of the proposition that the agent desires to be true, not by increasing the subjective probability of the negation of that proposition. That is why the causal connection between Bob's selective approach to evidence-gathering and his acquiring the belief that the bomb caused the crash counts as a deviant one. As the discussion of Bob's case indicates, a proper treatment of the problem of deviant causal chains in the present context would be a major undertaking, requiring careful investigation of a wide variety of "normal" routes to self-deception.

In brief, a protoanalysis of the focal concept in this section might take the following form: *S* enters self-deception in acquiring a belief that *p* if and only if *p* is false and *S* acquires the belief that *p* in "a suitably biased way." The preceding discussion suggests that the suitability at issue is a matter of kind of bias, degree of bias, and the nondeviance of causal connections between biasing processes and events, on the one hand, and the acquisition of the belief that *p*, on the other.

2. Parting Remarks

Defending a position on self-deception makes one wonder about one's results. Have I overestimated the merits of my own view or underestimated the merits of opposing views, owing to motivational or emotional biases? Are some of my arguments biased, owing perhaps to my having a stake in the truth of theses about self-deception that I have advocated in the past? I hope and believe that the answer to both questions is no, but readers should be the judges.

At least one commentator has interpreted earlier work of mine as defending the position that, in fact, there is no self-deception (Gibbins 1997, p. 115). That was not my intention then, nor is it now. I believe that self-deception is quite common, but I also believe that it is not properly conceptualized on the model of interpersonal deception and is not plausibly explained by "agency views." Some people will claim, on lexical or conceptual grounds, that if there is no intentional self-deception, or no self-deception involving the person's simultaneously believing that *p* and believing that ~*p* (the "dual-belief condition" discussed in ch. 4), then there is no self-deception at all. I hope that I am not self-deceived in finding my criticisms of the alleged lexical and conceptual underpinnings of this conditional claim persuasive.

I have not tried to prove here that there is no "strict" self-deception. Instead, I have offered an explanatory framework for accounting for garden-variety straight and twisted self-deception, and I have argued that, whereas there is considerable evidence for the existence of the processes and phenomena that I appealed to in constructing that framework, there is nothing approaching comparably weighty evidence for "dual beliefs" or the occurrence of unconscious attempts of the kinds that advocates of agency models of self-deception rely on. Despite my criticism of research purporting to demonstrate the existence of "strict" self-deception, including some quite ingenious experiments, I would welcome convincing evidence that such self-deception exists. Because its existence would have interesting implications about the human mind, I look forward to studying future efforts to produce powerful evidence for such self-deception.

Notes

Preface

1. The publisher of *Philosophical Psychology*, where Mele 1998a and 1999a appeared, is Taylor & Francis Ltd./Carfax/Routledge (http://www.tandf.co.uk).

Chapter 1
Introduction: Approaches, Puzzles, Biases, and Agency

1. See, e.g., Davidson 1985; Gur and Sackeim 1979; Haight 1980; Pears 1984; Quattrone and Tversky 1984; Trivers 1985.

2. On this case, see Barnes 1997, ch. 3; Dalgleish 1997, p. 110; Lazar 1999, pp. 274–77; and Pears 1984, pp. 42–44. Also see Davidson 1985, p. 144; Demos 1960, p. 589; McLaughlin 1988, p. 40; and Mele 1987a, pp. 114–18.

3. For this claim, see Bach 1981, p. 364; Siegler 1968, p. 161; and Szabados 1974, pp. 67–68.

4. For this more modest claim, see Gardiner 1970, p. 242; Johnston 1988, p. 67; Pears 1984, p. 42; and Sackeim and Gur 1985, p. 1365.

5. It is assumed here (and hereafter) that the substitution instances of both occurrences of *p* are represented in the same way. I forgo discussion of Kripke's puzzle about belief (Kripke 1979).

6. For a brief review of some literature on this puzzle, see Mele 1987b, pp. 4, 8.

7. One response is mental partitioning: the deceived part of the mind is unaware of what the deceiving part is up to. See Pears 1984 (cf. 1991) for a detailed response of this kind and Davidson 1985 (cf. 1982) for a more modest partitioning view. For criticism of some partitioning views of self-deception, see Johnston 1988; Mele 1987a, ch. 10; and Mele 1987b, pp. 3–6.

8. Incidentally, I understand degree of belief that *p* as a matter of degree of *confidence* that *p*. One who claims that all beliefs come in degrees in this sense is not committed to the idea that probabilities (from 0 to 1) enter into the *contents* of all beliefs.

9. Regarding the effects of motivation on time spent reading threatening information, see Baumeister and Cairns 1992.

10. Two uses of "motivate" should be distinguished. In one use, a desire's motivating a course of action or a belief is a matter of its *constituting* motivation for that course of action or belief. My desire to go fishing today constitutes motivation for me to go fishing, even if, desiring more to work on this chapter, I forgo a fishing trip. In another use, a desire motivates something only if it plays a role in *producing* that thing. In this book, I use "motivate" in the second sense.

11. On "time-lag" scenarios of this general kind, see Davidson 1985, p. 145; McLaughlin 1988, pp. 31–33; Mele 1983, pp. 374–75, 1987a, pp. 132–34; Sackeim 1988, p. 156; Sorensen 1985. In Mele 1983, drawing on Pascal, I describe a more realistic case in which an unhappy atheist, convinced that he would be much better off believing in God, consciously sets out to cause himself to believe that God exists by attending religious services, associating with religious people, and the like (pp. 374–75). Assume the following: he eventually succeeds; there is no God; and his evidence provides greater warrant for God's nonexistence than for God's existence. In that case, I claim, this agent deceives himself and is self-deceived.

12. Some readers may be attracted to the view that although Ike deceives himself, this is not self-deception at all (cf. Audi 1997; Barnes 1997, pp. 110–17; Davidson 1985, p. 145; McLaughlin 1988). Imagine that Ike had been embarrassed by his performance in class that day and consciously viewed the remark as ironic when he wrote it. Imagine also that Ike strongly desires to see himself as exceptionally intelligent and that this desire helps to explain his writing the sentence. If, in this scenario, Ike later came to believe that he was brilliant in class that day

on the basis of a subsequent reading of his diary, would many such readers be more inclined to view the case as one of self-deception?

13. Pears 1991 reacts to the charge of incoherence, responding to Johnston 1988.

14. On the motivating of an intentional *A*-ing by an intrinsic desire to *A*, see Mele 1992, ch. 6.

Chapter 2
Garden-Variety Straight Self-Deception: Some Psychological Processes

1. Cf. Mele 1983, pp. 369–70. Cf. Bach 1981, pp. 358–61, on "rationalization" and "evasion"; Baron 1988, pp. 258, 275–76, on positive and negative misinterpretation and "selective exposure"; and Greenwald 1988 on various kinds of "avoidance." For other routes to self-deception, including what is sometimes called "immersion," see Mele 1987a, pp. 149–51, 157–58. On self-handicapping, another potential route to self-deception, see Higgins, Snyder, and Berglas 1990.

2. Literature on "selective exposure" is reviewed in Frey 1986. Frey defends the reality of *motivated* selective evidence-gathering, arguing that a host of data is best accommodated by a variant of Festinger's (1957, 1964) cognitive dissonance theory.

3. If, in the way I described, Betty acquires or retains the false belief that her boss is not sexist, it is natural to count her as self-deceived. This is so even if, owing to her motivationally biased evidence-gathering, the evidence that she actually *possesses* does not weigh more heavily in support of the proposition that her boss is sexist than against it. I return to this issue in Chapter 3, section 1.

4. For a challenge to studies of the vividness effect, see Taylor and Thompson 1982. They contend that research on the issue has been flawed in various ways, but that studies conducted in "situations that reflect the informational competition found in everyday life" might "show the existence of a strong vividness effect" (pp. 178–79).

5. This theme is developed in Mele 1987a, ch. 10 in explaining the occurrence of self-deception. Kunda 1990 develops the same theme, paying particular attention to evidence that motivation sometimes

triggers the confirmation bias. Cf. Silver, Sabini, and Miceli 1989, p. 222.

6. For motivational interpretations of the confirmation bias, see Frey 1986, pp. 70–74; Friedrich 1993; and Trope and Liberman 1996, pp. 252–65.

7. Friedrich uses the expression "subjectively important errors" (1993, p. 300).

8. There is some ambiguity about hypothesis *rejection* in the paper. The passages I quoted from Trope and Liebeman 1996, p. 253, support the interpretation I offered, as do some others. However, Trope and Liberman also write: "in statistical decision making, the decision criterion for accepting a hypothesis is conventionally set much more strictly than the criterion for rejecting it" (p. 254). Here, "rejecting" a hypothesis *p* seems to be synonymous with "not accepting" (or not believing that) *p*. And, of course, one who does not accept or believe that *p* might not believe that ~*p* either. Having no evidence about the current weather in Beijing, I neither believe that it is raining there nor believe that it is not raining there.

9. I am also content to use their terms "false acceptance" and "false rejection," even though it is not the acceptance or rejection that is false but the proposition accepted or rejected.

10. Friedrich is not entirely consistent about this. He says that there are situations in which "no particular error is viewed as primary or important" by a hypothesis tester (1993, p. 305). In personal correspondence, Friedrich indicated that the passage I just quoted from p. 300 is an overstatement.

11. Trope and Liberman allow for unmotivated cognitive biases in hypothesis testing (1996, p. 260).

12. Indeed, Friedrich himself suggests at one point (1993, p. 305) that "plausibility testing" is a "default" strategy. Examples of plausibility testing are testing the hypothesis that "people higher in the trait of extraversion make better salespeople" by checking to see whether "people high in the hypothesized characteristic of extraversion . . . turned out to be high in the target quality of performance" (p. 299) or by doing "a cursory scan for co-occurrences" of high extraversion and high performance (p. 305). (Notice that if people lower in extraversion were even better salespeople, these tests would not detect that.)

13. Friedrich does grant at one point that "People may . . . be able to ignore primary-error-driven preferences at times and apply normative rules" (1993, p. 317), mentioning in a note (n. 11) that some of Gigerenzer and Hug's (1992) "subjects (several mathematics and natural science majors) indicated that they were able—with some difficulty—to ignore cheater detection concerns and apply formal truth-table rules to all the social-contract problems they received."

Chapter 3
Self-Deception without Puzzles

1. People may be deceived *into* believing something that they are not deceived *in* believing (cf. Mele 1987a, pp. 127–28). *A* might execute a tricky plan for deceiving *B* into believing something that, unbeknownst to *A*, is true. And *A* might thereby cause *B* to believe this proposition, *p*. Since *p* is true, *B* is not deceived *in* believing it. Even so, it is plausible that *A* deceived *B into* believing it, if *A* caused *B* to believe that *p* partly by deceiving him into believing some false propositions suggestive of *p*.

2. See the block quotations from Pears 1984 and Davidson 1985 toward the end of chapter 1.

3. This is not to deny that self-deceivers sometimes believe that *p* while being aware that their evidence favors ~*p*. On such cases, see Mele 1987a, ch. 8 and pp. 135–36.

4. My discussion of Barnes's position derives partly from my review of her book (Mele 1999b).

5. For purposes of stylistic uniformity, I have substituted "~*q*" for Barnes's "not-*q*."

6. If self-deception is best explained partly in terms of our tendency to test hypotheses in ways that minimize "crucial errors," the kind of anxiety reduction on which Barnes insists—that is, reducing the anxiety that one is presently feeling—is not the only issue, for crucial errors are not limited to errors that would fail to reduce present anxiety. For example, errors that can reasonably be expected to *produce* psychological discomfort are quite relevant. Moreover, such errors are possible

for people who are not presently feeling anxious about the relevant topic. (Dion Scott-Kakures [n.d.], focusing on twisted self-deception, advances a powerful critique of Barnes's claim that the purpose of self-deception is to reduce anxiety.)

7. I comment on a case of this kind in Mele 1987a, p. 130.

8. I also mentioned a second static puzzle, according to which self-deception requires simultaneously having and lacking the belief that *p*. It rests on a stronger assumption that I criticized in Chapter 1.

9. Pears identifies what I have called internal biasing and input-control strategies and treats "acting as if something were so in order to generate the belief that it is so" as a third strategy (1984, p. 61).

10. The condition of Gordon's staff is analogous to that of the agent in an example that Talbott explores in this connection (1995, pp. 60–62). A man has significant grounds for thinking that his car might need new brakes; and, naturally, he hopes that the brakes are fine, given the expense of replacing them. Despite this hope, he comes to believe that his brakes are failing. But notice that the cost of his falsely believing that his brakes are fine (great personal danger) is considerably higher than the cost of his falsely believing that they are failing.

11. Talbott suggests that there are different preference rankings in the two kinds of case. (The preferences need not be objects of awareness, of course.) In cases of self-deception, the agents' highest relevant preference is that they believe "that *p* is true, if *p* is true"; and their second-highest preference is that they believe "that *p* is true, if *p* is false"—self-deceiving agents want to believe that *p* is true *whether or not* it is true. In the contrasting cases, agents have the same highest preference, but the self-deceiver's second-highest preference is the *lowest* preference of these agents: these agents have a higher-ranking preference "*not* to believe that *p*, if *p* is false." Suppose, for the sake of argument, that this diagnosis of the difference between the two kinds of case is correct. Why should we hold that in order to account for the target difference—namely, that in one case there is a motivated biasing of data and in the other there is not—we must suppose that an intention to deceive oneself (or to get oneself to believe that *p*, or to make it easier for oneself to believe that *p*) is at work in one case but not in the other? Given our understanding of various ways in which motivation can bias cognition in the absence of such an intention, we can understand how one preference ranking can do this while another does

not. An agent with the second preference ranking may have strong motivation to ascertain whether *p* is true or false; and that may block any tendency toward motivated biasing of relevant data. This would not be true of an agent with the first preference ranking.

12. As I pointed out in Chapter 1, section 2, those who prefer to think in terms of degree of belief should read such expressions of mine as "*S* believes that *p*" as shorthand for "*S* believes that *p* to a degree greater than 0.5 (on a scale from 0 to 1)."

Chapter 4
Attempted Empirical Demonstrations of Strict Self-Deception

1. Notice that simultaneously believing that *p* and believing that ~*p*—that is, *Bp* & *B~p*—is distinguishable from believing the *conjunction* of the two propositions: *B*(*p* & ~*p*). We do not always put two and two together. Also, it is assumed that the element common to *p* and ~*p* is represented in the same way (see ch. 1, n. 5).

2. See Demos 1960; Foss 1980; Gur and Sackeim 1979; Haight 1980; Kipp 1980; Paluch 1967; Quattrone and Tversky 1984; Sackeim and Gur 1978, 1985; Siegler 1968; and Trivers 1985.

3. Setting aside self-deception, one might think that situations featuring habitual behavior of a certain kind are promising locations for "dual beliefs." People who wear a watch almost every day, as I do, are in the habit of checking it when they want to know the time. The habit is not quite as simple as this description suggests, of course. I never wear a watch when I play racquetball, and sometimes, after a game, I want to know whether I have time for another game. But I do not then look at my left wrist (where I wear my watch). One might take this to indicate that my watch-checking habit is, more fully described, a habit of looking at my left wrist when I want to know the time and believe that my watch is there. Now, on rare occasions, I forget to wear my watch. I leave it at home on an otherwise ordinary day. On such a day, sitting in my office and wanting to know the time, I may look at my left wrist. I may do this a few times during the day, even though I have learned that my watch is not in its ordinary place. (After a while, I catch myself when I am about to look and I find what I was about

to do somewhat amusing.) One might suppose that my habit-driven behavior shows that I believe that I am wearing my watch. One might suppose, as well, that because I have learned that I am not wearing it, I also believe, at the same time, that I am not wearing it. Again, I have not claimed that simultaneously believing that *p* and believing that ~*p* is conceptually or psychologically impossible. I have no theoretical need to insist that "dual beliefs" are absent in the present scenario. Perhaps the two different beliefs are stored in two different mental compartments. But I am not convinced that this is so. The operative habit may be the habit of looking at my left wrist when I want to know the time and am in situations in which I normally wear a watch (and find it convenient to look at my left wrist). That habit need not involve a belief that my watch is on my wrist. The same is true of a habit that includes the conditions just mentioned and the further condition of lacking a salient belief that I am not wearing my watch. (Alternatively, I may just keep forgetting that I am not wearing my watch.)

4. For purposes of stylistic uniformity, I have substituted "~*p*" for Sackeim and Gur's "not-*p*."

5. The claim that there are nonintentional acts of decision would be rejected by some philosophers as conceptually incoherent. See, e.g., McCann 1986a.

6. In a later essay, Sackeim grants this (1988, pp. 161–62).

7. He also suggests that they may be "unaware of . . . the discrepancy between the two beliefs" (cf. Bermudez 1997).

8. Quattrone and Tversky took steps to reduce the likelihood that subjects would lie to impress the experimenters. Subjects were told that only *shifts* in tolerance would indicate heart types and that neither the experimenter present during the first trial nor the one administering the second trial would know the results of the other trial. The experimenter at the second trial was presented as a secretary who "knew nothing of the study's hypotheses, description, or rationale" (1984, p. 24). And the questionnaires were filled out anonymously.

9. As this implies, in challenging the claim that the sincere deniers have the belief at issue, I am not challenging the popular idea that attempts are explained at least partly in terms of pertinent beliefs and desires.

10. Obviously, whether the subjects satisfy the conditions offered in Chapter 3, section 1, as sufficient for self-deception depends on

the relative strength of their evidence for the pertinent pair of propositions.

11. The relative costs would depend partly on their beliefs about what can be done to cure heart disease and about coping measures. Also, we might expect subjects with no prior indications of heart disease to respond differently than hypothetical subjects with significant prior evidence that they have heart problems.

12. The same point applies to his threshold for believing that his present pain is as intense as the pain he assigned a "10" on the first trial, as compared with his threshold for believing that his present pain is less intense than that earlier pain.

13. Cf. the point about interpreting facial expressions in chapter 2, section 1.

14. It is interesting that Trope and his coauthors (Trope et al. 1997, p. 122) assume, unnecessarily, that Quattrone and Tversky's subjects were "making an effort" to adjust their tolerance.

15. Similar questions have been raised about partitioning hypotheses that fall short of postulating multiple personalities. See, e.g., Johnston 1988 and Sorensen 1985.

Chapter 5
Twisted Self-Deception

1. H. H. Price writes that in Victorian novels, "ladies acknowledged a moral obligation to believe that their husbands and fiancés were impeccably virtuous" and that some have "held that there was a moral obligation to believe that all the members of one's family were persons of the highest excellence, or at least of great excellence" (1954, pp. 13–14). Many people may hold beliefs that are consistent with the seemingly more reasonable principle that it is best not to believe ill of members of one's family, unless and until one has overwhelming evidence of wrongdoing on their part. Many of the same people may hold beliefs that are consistent with a considerably less generous principle about believing ill of people to whom they have no special ties. This is not to say, of course, that many people explicitly accept principles of these kinds. An aversion to psychological discomfort may contribute significantly to the explanation of the tendency to give the benefit of the doubt to loved ones.

2. Dalgleish 1997 explicitly suggests this.

3. See, e.g., Butler and Mathews 1983; Derryberry 1988, 1991; Kitayama and Howard 1994; Klinger 1996; and Tesser, Pilkington, and McInstosh 1989.

4. For a review of the "mood congruity effect," see Blaney 1986.

5. On *anxiety* that ~*p* in this connection, see Johnston 1988 and Barnes 1997.

6. See, e.g., Davis 1988 and Lyons 1980, p. 64.

7. This is a major theme in Johnston 1988 and Barnes 1997. Cf. Tesser et al. 1989.

8. I defend this thesis in Mele 1995, ch. 6. In this paragraph I borrow from p. 106 of that chapter.

9. For an instructive review, see Kunda 1990. On the effectiveness of various incentives for increased accuracy, see Trope and Liberman 1996, pp. 254–56. (In this paragraph, I borrow from Mele 1995, p. 97.)

10. Knight also discusses what appears to be a putative straight case (1988, p. 184).

11. It is worth asking why people would persist in using cognitive strategies that they not only "should know are biased" but in fact deem biased. There are a variety of possibilities. One is that some people judge that common heuristics, even though they are not perfectly reliable, are perfectly suitable for ordinary use. They may believe that more reliable but more time-consuming strategies should be reserved for special cases where the stakes are relatively high. When such people, unconsciously using such heuristics, arrive at false beliefs that have no particular motivational or emotional significance for them, a charge of self-deception is excessive.

12. A referee suggested that this test is unfair to atheists, since the great majority of (actual) observers would be theists. However, that eligible observers be *impartial* is an important constraint. My guess is that at most a tiny percentage of theists have no motivational stake in theism's being true.

13. I have noticed some confusion about the usage of "jealousy"' in ordinary speech. If one is jealous because one's husband is flirting with another woman, is one jealous of one's husband or the other woman? De Sousa expresses the proper usage succinctly: "the person one is jealous *of* plays an entirely different part in one's jealousy from that of the rival *because of whom* one is jealous" (1987, p. 75).

14. In Jeff's case, as in many cases, the desire may be, more precisely, for close and *exclusive* romantic attachment.

15. Contributions of emotion to self-deception that are not "direct" merit mention too. A woman's *love* for her husband, or her *fear* that she cannot get along without him, may make a significant causal contribution to her desiring that he not be having an affair and, thereby, to her self-deception about this. If that desire increases the salience of her apparent evidence of his fidelity or helps to determine her relevant confidence thresholds, emotions that contribute to the desire play an indirect part in this. Emotions might also play a part in explaining some instances of self-deception by weakening one's motivation to assess evidence carefully, thereby increasing the probability that one's beliefs will be unduly influenced by one's desires. Grief and sadness may do this.

References

Adams, F. 1986. "Intention and Intentional Action: The Simple View." *Mind and Language* 1:281–301.

Adams, F., and A. Mele. 1992. "The Intention/Volition Debate." *Canadian Journal of Philosophy* 22:323–38.

Audi, R. 1982. "Self-Deception, Action, and Will." *Erkenntnis* 18: 133–58.

———. 1997. "Self-Deception vs. Self-Caused Deception: A Comment on Professor Mele." *Behavioral and Brain Sciences* 20:104.

Bach, K. 1981. "An Analysis of Self-Deception." *Philosophy and Phenomenological Research* 41:351–70.

———. 1997. "Thinking and Believing in Self-Deception." *Behavioral and Brain Sciences* 20:105.

———. 1998. "(Apparent) Paradoxes of Self-Deception and Decision." In J. Dupuy, ed., *Self-Deception and Paradoxes of Rationality*, pp. 163–89. Cambridge: Cambridge University Press.

Barnes, A. 1997. *Seeing through Self-Deception*. Cambridge: Cambridge University Press.

Baron, J. 1988. *Thinking and Deciding*. Cambridge: Cambridge University Press.

Baumeister, R., and K. Cairns. 1992. "Repression and Self-Presentation: When Audiences Interfere with Self-Deceptive Strategies." *Journal of Personality and Social Psychology* 62:851–62.

Baumeister, R., and L. Newman. 1994. "Self-Regulation of Cognitive Inference and Decision Processes." *Personality and Social Psychology Bulletin* 20:3–19.

Bem, D. 1972. "Self-Perception Theory." *Advances in Experimental Social Psychology* 6:1–62.

Bermudez, J. 1997. "Defending Intentionalist Accounts of Self-Deception." *Behavioral and Brain Sciences* 20:107–8.

Blaney, P. 1986. "Affect and Memory: A Review." *Psychological Bulletin* 99:229–46.

Bratman, M. 1987. *Intention, Plans, and Practical Reason*. Cambridge: Harvard University Press.

Brown, J., and K. Dutton. 1995. "Truth and Consequences: The Costs and Benefits of Accurate Self-Knowledge." *Personality and Social Psychology Bulletin* 21:1288–96.

Brown, S., and D. Kenrick. 1997. "Paradoxical Self-Deception: Maybe Not So Paradoxical after All." *Behavioral and Brain Sciences* 20:109–10.

Butler, G., and A. Mathews. 1983. "Cognitive Processes in Anxiety." *Advances in Behavioral Research and Therapy* 5:51–62.

Chodoff, P., S. Friedman, and D. Hamburg. 1964. "Stress, Defenses and Coping Behavior: Observations in Parents of Children with Malignant Disease." *American Journal of Psychiatry* 120:743–49.

Dalgleish, T. 1997. "Once More with Feeling: The Role of Emotion in Self-Deception." *Behavioral and Brain Sciences* 20:110–11.

Davidson, D. 1982. "Paradoxes of Irrationality." In R. Wollheim and J. Hopkins, eds., *Philosophical Essays on Freud*, pp. 289–305. Cambridge: Cambridge University Press.

———. 1985. "Deception and Division." In E. LePore and B. McLaughlin, eds., *Actions and Events*, pp. 138–48. Oxford: Basil Blackwell.

Davis, W. 1988. "A Causal Theory of Experiential Fear." *Canadian Journal of Philosophy* 18:459–83.

Demos, R. 1960. "Lying to Oneself." *Journal of Philosophy* 57:588–95.

Derryberry, D. 1988. "Emotional Influences on Evaluative Judgments: Roles of Arousal, Attention, and Spreading Activation." *Motivation and Emotion* 12:23–55.

———. 1991. "The Immediate Effects of Positive and Negative Feedback Signals." *Journal of Personality and Social Psychology* 61:267–78.

de Sousa, R. 1987. *The Rationality of Emotion*. Cambridge: MIT Press.

Douglas, W., and K. Gibbins. 1983. "Inadequacy of Voice Recognition as a Demonstration of Self-Deception." *Journal of Personality and Social Psychology* 44:589–92.

Farrell, D. 1980. "Jealousy." *Philosophical Review* 89:527–59.

Festinger, L. 1957. *A Theory of Cognitive Dissonance*. Stanford: Stanford University Press.

———. 1964. *Conflict, Decision, and Dissonance*. Stanford: Stanford University Press.

Foss, J. 1980. "Rethinking Self-Deception." *American Philosophical Quarterly* 17:237–43.

———. 1997. "How Many Beliefs Can Dance in the Head of the Self-Deceived?" *Behavioral and Brain Sciences* 20:111–12.

Frey, D. 1986. "Recent Research on Selective Exposure to Information." In L. Berkowitz, ed., *Advances in Experimental Social Psychology*, pp. 41–80, New York: Academic Press.

Friedrich, J. 1993. "Primary Error Detection and Minimization (PEDMIN) Strategies in Social Cognition: A Reinterpretation of Confirmation Bias Phenomena." *Psychological Review* 100:298–319.

Gardiner, P. 1970. "Error, Faith, and Self-Deception." *Proceedings of the Aristotelian Society* 70:221–43.

Gergen, K. 1985. "The Ethnopsychology of Self-Deception." In M. Martin, ed., *Self-Deception and Self-Understanding*, pp. 228–43. Lawrence: University of Kansas Press.

Gibbins, K. 1997. "Partial Belief as a Solution to the Logical Problem of Holding Simultaneous, Contrary Beliefs in Self-Deception Research." *Behavioral and Brain Sciences* 20:115–16.

Gibbins, K., and W. Douglas. 1985. "Voice Recognition and Self-Deception: A Reply to Sackeim and Gur." *Journal of Personality and Social Psychology* 48:1369–72.

Gigerenzer, G., and K. Hug. 1992. "Domain-Specific Reasoning: Social Contracts, Cheating, and Perspective Change." *Cognition* 43:127–71.

Gilovich, T. 1991. *How We Know What Isn't So*. New York: Macmillan.

Gorassini, D. 1997. "Intentional Self-Deception Can and Does Occur." *Behavioral and Brain Sciences* 20:116.

Greenwald, A. 1988. "Self-Knowledge and Self-Deception." In J. Lockard and D. Paulhus, eds., *Self-Deception: An Adaptive Mechanism?*, pp. 113–31. Englewood Cliffs, N.J.: Prentice-Hall.

Gur, R., and H. Sackeim. 1979. "Self-Deception: A Concept in Search of a Phenomenon." *Journal of Personality and Social Psychology* 37:147–69.

Haight, M. 1980. *A Study of Self-Deception*. Sussex: Harvester Press.

Harman, G. 1976. "Practical Reasoning." *Review of Metaphysics* 79:431–63. Reprinted in A. Mele, ed., *The Philosophy of Action*, pp. 149–77. Oxford: Oxford University Press, 1997.

———. 1986. *Change in View.* Cambridge: MIT Press.

Higgins, R., C. Snyder, and S. Berglas. 1990. *Self-Handicapping: The Paradox That Isn't.* New York: Plenum Press.

Johnston, M. 1988. "Self-Deception and the Nature of Mind." In B. McLaughlin and A. Rorty, eds., *Perspectives on Self-Deception*, pp. 63–91. Berkeley: University of California Press.

Kipp, D. 1980. "On Self-Deception." *Philosophical Quarterly* 30:305–17.

Kirsch, I. 1997. "Hypnotic Responding and Self-Deception." *Behavioral and Brain Sciences* 20:118–19.

Kitayama, S., and S. Howard. 1994. "Affective Regulation of Perception and Comprehension: Amplification and Semantic Priming." In P. Niedenthal and S. Kitayama, eds., *The Heart's Eye*, pp. 41–65. New York: Academic Press.

Klayman, J., and Y.-W. Ha. 1987. "Confirmation, Disconfirmation, and Information in Hypothesis Testing." *Psychological Review* 94:211–28.

Klinger, E. 1996. "Emotional Influences on Cognitive Processing, with Implications for Theories of Both." In P. Gollwitzer and J. Bargh, eds., *The Psychology of Action*, pp. 168–89. New York: Guilford Press.

Knight, M. 1988. "Cognitive and Motivational Bases of Self-Deception: Commentary on Mele's Irrationality." *Philosophical Psychology* 1:179–88.

Koriat, A., R. Melkman, J. Averill, and R. Lazarus. 1972. "The Self-Control of Emotional Reactions to a Stressful Film." *Journal of Personality* 40:601–19.

Kripke, S. 1979. "A Puzzle about Belief." In A. Margalit, ed., *Meaning and Use*, pp. 239–83. Dordrecht: Reidel.

Kruglanski, A. 1989. *Lay Epistemics and Human Knowledge*. New York: Plenum Press.

Kunda, Z. 1987. "Motivated Inference: Self-Serving Generation and Evaluation of Causal Theories." *Journal of Personality and Social Psychology* 53:636–47.

———. 1990. "The Case for Motivated Reasoning." *Psychological Bulletin* 108:480–98.

Lazar, A. 1997. "Self-Deception and the Desire to Believe." *Behavioral and Brain Sciences* 20:119–20.

———. 1999. "Deceiving Oneself or Self-Deceived? On the Formation of Beliefs 'Under the Influence.' " *Mind* 108: 265–90.

Liberman, A., and S. Chaiken. 1992. "Defensive Processing of Personally Relevant Health Messages." *Personality and Social Psychology Bulletin* 18:669–79.

Losonsky, M. 1997. "Self-Deceivers' Intentions and Possessions." *Behavioral and Brain Sciences* 20:121–22.

Lyons, W. 1980. *Emotion*. Cambridge: Cambridge University Press.

Martin, M. 1997. "Self-Deceiving Intentions." *Behavioral and Brain Sciences* 20:122–23.

McCann, H. 1986a. "Intrinsic Intentionality." *Theory and Decision* 20:247–73.

———. 1986b. "Rationality and the Range of Intention." *Midwest Studies in Philosophy* 10:191–211.

———. 1991. "Settled Objectives and Rational Constraints." *American Philosophical Quarterly* 28:25–36. Reprinted in A. Mele, ed., *The Philosophy of Action*, pp. 204–22. Oxford: Oxford University Press, 1997.

McLaughlin, B. 1988. "Exploring the Possibility of Self-Deception in Belief." In B. McLaughlin and A. Rorty, eds., *Perspectives on Self-Deception*, pp. 29–62. Berkeley: University of California Press.

Mele, A. 1982. "Self-Deception, Action, and Will: Comments." *Erkenntnis* 18:159–64.

———. 1983. "Self-Deception." *Philosophical Quarterly* 33:365–77.

———. 1987a. *Irrationality*. New York: Oxford University Press.

———. 1987b. "Recent Work on Self-Deception." *American Philosophical Quarterly* 24:1–17.

———. 1992. *Springs of Action*. New York: Oxford University Press.

———. 1995. *Autonomous Agents*. New York: Oxford University Press.

———. 1997a. "Real Self-Deception." *Behavioral and Brain Sciences* 20:91–102.

Mele, A.. 1997b. "Understanding and Explaining Real Self-Deception." *Behavioral and Brain Sciences* 20:127–34.

———. 1998a. "Motivated Belief and Agency." *Philosophical Psychology* 11:353–69.

———. 1998b. "Two Paradoxes of Self-Deception." In J. Dupuy, ed., *Self-Deception and Paradoxes of Rationality*, pp. 37–58. Stanford: CSLI.

———. 1999a. "Twisted Self-Deception." *Philosophical Psychology* 12: 117–37.

———. 1999b. Review of Barnes 1997. *Philosophical Psychology* 12: 104–7.

Mele, A., and P. Moser. 1994. "Intentional Action." *Noûs* 28: 39–68. Reprinted in A. Mele, ed., *The Philosophy of Action*, pp. 223–55. Oxford: Oxford University Press, 1997.

Mele, A., and S. Sverdlik. 1996. "Intention, Intentional Action, and Moral Responsibility." *Philosophical Studies* 82:265–87.

Nisbett, R., and L. Ross. 1980. *Human Inference: Strategies and Shortcomings of Social Judgment*. Englewood Cliffs, N.J.: Prentice-Hall.

O'Shaughnessy, B. 1980. *The Will*. Vol. 2. Cambridge: Cambridge University Press.

Paluch, S. 1967. "Self-Deception." *Inquiry* 10:268–78.

Peacocke, C. 1985. "Intention and *Akrasia*." In B. Vermazen and M. Hintikka, eds., *Essays on Davidson*, pp. 51–73. Oxford: Clarendon Press.

Pears, D. 1984. *Motivated Irrationality*. Oxford: Oxford University Press.

———. 1991. "Self-Deceptive Belief-Formation. *Synthese* 89:393–405.

Peele, S. 1989. *Diseasing of America: Addiction Treatment Out of Control*. Lexington, Ky.: Lexington Books.

Perring, C. 1997. "Direct, Fully Intentional Self-Deception Is Also Real." *Behavioral and Brain Sciences* 20:123–24.

Price, H. 1954. "Belief and Will." *Aristotelian Society* (suppl. vol.) 28: 1–26.

Quattrone, G., and A. Tversky. 1984. "Causal versus Diagnostic Contingencies: On Self-Deception and on the Voter's Illusion." *Journal of Personality and Social Psychology* 46:237–48.

Rorty, A. 1988. "The Deceptive Self: Liars, Layers, and Lairs." In B. McLaughlin and A. Rorty, eds., *Perspectives on Self-Deception*, pp. 11–28. Berkeley: University of California Press.

Sackeim, H. 1988. "Self-Deception: A Synthesis." In J. Lockard and D. Paulhus, eds., *Self-Deception: An Adaptive Mechanism?*, pp. 146–65. Englewood Cliffs, N.J.: Prentice-Hall.

Sackeim, H., and R. Gur. 1978. "Self-Deception, Self-Confrontation, and Consciousness." In G. Schwartz and D. Shapiro, eds., *Consciousness and Self-Regulation*, 2:139–97. New York: Plenum Press.

———. 1985. "Voice Recognition and the Ontological Status of Self-Deception." *Journal of Personality and Social Psychology* 48:1365–68.

———. 1997. "Flavors of Self-Deception: Ontology and Epidemiology." *Behavioral and Brain Sciences* 20:125–26.

Scott-Kakures, D. (N.d.). "Anxiety and Interest in Self-Deception." Manuscript, 1999.

Sharpsteen, D., and L. Kirkpatrick. 1997. "Romantic Jealousy and Adult Romantic Attachment." *Journal of Personality and Social Psychology* 72:627–40.

Siegler, F. 1968. "An Analysis of Self-Deception." *Noûs* 2:147–64.

Silver, M., J. Sabini, and M. Miceli. 1989. "On Knowing Self-Deception." *Journal for the Theory of Social Behaviour* 19:213–27.

Singer, I. 1953. *Gimpel the Fool and Other Short Stories*. New York: Noonday Press.

Skinner, B. F. 1953. *Science and Human Behavior*. New York: Macmillan.

Sorensen, R. 1985. "Self-Deception and Scattered Events." *Mind* 94: 64–69.

Szabados, B. 1974. "Self-Deception." *Canadian Journal of Philosophy* 4:51–68.

———. 1985. "The Self, Its Passions, and Self-Deception." In M. Martin, ed., *Self-Deception and Self-Understanding*, pp. 143–68. Lawrence: University of Kansas Press.

Talbott, W. 1995. "Intentional Self-Deception in a Single, Coherent Self." *Philosophy and Phenomenological Research* 55:27–74.

———. 1997. "Does Self-Deception Involve Intentional Biasing?" *Behavioral and Brain Sciences* 20:127.

Taylor, S., and S. Fiske. 1975. "Point of View and Perceptions of Causality." *Journal of Personality and Social Psychology* 32:439–45.

Taylor, S. 1978. "Salience, Attention and Attribution: Top of the Head Phenomena." In L. Berkowitz, ed., *Advances in Experimental Social Psychology*, 11:250–88. New York: Academic Press.

Taylor, S., and S. Thompson. 1982. "Stalking the Elusive 'Vividness' Effect." *Psychological Review* 89:155–81.

Tesser, A., C. Pilkington, and W. McIntosh. 1989. "Self-Evaluation Maintenance and the Mediational Role of Emotion: The Perception of Friends and Strangers." *Journal of Personality and Social Psychology* 57:442–56.

Tice, D., and R. Baumeister. 1993. "Controlling Anger: Self-Induced Emotion Change." In D. Wegner and J. Pennebaker, eds., *Handbook of Mental Control*, pp. 393–409. Englewood Cliffs, N.J.: Prentice-Hall.

Trivers, R. 1985. *Social Evolution*. Menlo Park, Calif.: Benjamin/Cummings.

Trope, Y., B. Gervey, B. and N. Liberman. 1997. "Wishful Thinking from a Pragmatic Hypothesis-Testing Perspective." In M. Myslobodsky, ed., *The Mythomanias: The Nature of Deception and Self-Deception*, pp. 105–31. Mahwah, N.J.: Lawrence Erlbaum.

Trope, Y., and A. Liberman. 1996. "Social Hypothesis Testing: Cognitive and Motivational Mechanisms." In E. Higgins and A. Kruglanski, eds., *Social Psychology: Handbook of Basic Principles*, pp. 239–70. New York: Guilford Press.

Tversky, A., and D. Kahnemann. 1973. "Availability: A Heuristic for Judging Frequency and Probability." *Cognitive Psychology* 5:207–32.

Weiskrantz, L. 1986. *Blindsight: A Case Study and Implications*. Oxford: Oxford University Press.

Index

Made in the USA
Lexington, KY
07 May 2015